WALKING ON THE WIND

MICHAEL GARRETT

BEAR & COMPANY
PUBLISHING
ROCHESTER, VERMONT

LIBRARY OF CONGRESS CATALOGING-IN-PUBLICATION DATA

Garrett, Michael Tlanusta, 1970–
  Walking on the wind : Cherokee teachings for healing through harmony
and balance / Michael Garrett.
      p. cm.
  Includes bibliographical references.
  ISBN 1-879181-49-5
  1. Cherokee Indians—Religion. 2. Cherokee Indians—Medicine.
3. Indians of North America—Religion. 4. Indians of North America—
Medicine. I. Title.
E99.C5G24 1998
299'.7855—dc21   98–11075
                                                                        CIP

Bear & Company, Inc.
Rochester, Vermont
Bear & Company is a division of Inner Traditions International
www.InnerTraditions.com

Cover art © 1998 by Francene Hart
Cover and interior page design: Melinda Belter
Interior illustrations: Debi Duke and Francene Hart
Editing: Barbara Doern Drew
Printed in the United States

9 8 7

Contents

For my family, for "the people," and for all those
who breathe the breath of life
with the wonder of a child. Keep smiling.
It *is* beautiful, isn't it?
Osda Nuwati.

Acknowledgments

I have been blessed with a mother and father, Phyllis and J.T. Garrett, who always did their best to answer my questions and teach me how to live and love and learn, despite my habit of just "wandering off" in my own direction. They have encouraged me in times of hardship and shared in times of joy. They brought me into this world, and I am thankful to the wind for giving me the breath of life. I thank my sister, Melissa, for showing me the difference between boys and girls, between brother and sister, and for helping me to see that even though they are very different, there is and always will be a love between the two that requires no words.

I thank my grandma Ruth Rogers Garrett for showing me the lighter side of everything, reminding me to never take myself too seriously and to never let anyone else fail to take me seriously. I thank my late grandfather Jasper Thomas Garrett Sr. for teaching me what it means to be truly strong, not so much in body but in the absolute clarity of mind and spirit. I thank my grandma Miriam and grandpa Reverend Al Riter for always being proud and supportive of everyone they love and for showing me the importance of touching people's lives.

I thank my aunt Barbara for reminding me to laugh and to look beyond the surface; I thank my aunt Patsy for showing me the meaning of a true teacher and how important it is to live the words. I thank my uncle John for teaching me how important it is to dream; I thank my uncle Jim for showing me the importance of wit and calm.

I thank my cousins Joey Owle and Brian Owle; my

cousins Jimmy and Jeff Riter; my family and friends Grady Garrett, Donna Riter, Eric Riter, Emily Riter, Kim Riter, Harry Page, Dr. Carol Locust, Dr. Nate Mayfield, Pat and Bernard DeAsis, John and Peggy Sill, Ruth and Lonnie Revels (and all those at the Guilford Native American Association), Neal Coulter, Jamie Hummingbird, Dirk Welch, Paula Maney Nelson, Tommy and David Wachacha, Tony Neal, Ly Peang-Meth, Lynn Gonzalez, Jon Sill, Shannon Dwyer, Derenda Wiemer, Charlene Gonnie, Lori B. Crutchfield, Pam Brott, Tania Castillero, Bernd Burwitz, Keith Davis, Simon and Alexsis Ferguson, Lynda and Mike Ruf, Dale and Jeannie Stacy, Sharon Begaye, Shirley Limbara, Nelsa Webber, Barney Singer, Rebecca and Bear Van Der Goot, Bryan Smith, Marisa Taylor, Rebecca Panek, Michael Wilbur, Edil Torres, and Jim Frank.

I thank my mentors and teachers (extended family who have moved me beyond myself) Mrs. Hodges, Mrs. Baker, Mrs. Harvey, Sandy Puckett, Mr. Sink, Ms. Casey, Sonia Paslawsky, Chuck Dormo, Dr. Juanita Anders, Robert Malloy, Debra Robinson, Dr. Chuck Oglesby, Dr. George McCoy, Dr. Tracy Robinson, Joseph Iron Eye Dudley, Dr. Lynn Karmel, Pamela Wilson, Betty Byron, Dr. Jane Myers, Dr. Tom Sweeney, Dr. Willie Baber, Dr. John Hattie, Dr. Bob Barret, and Dr. Mary Thomas Burke. I thank our beloved Cherokee elders and teachers Myrtle Driver Johnson, Richard Teesateskie, Driver Pheasant, Gil Jackson, Ray Kinsland, Roberta and Daniel Walkingstick, Robert and Jean Bushyhead and many, many others, as well as all of our elders at Tsali Manor.

I thank the sunshine for teaching me that there is no light without the darkness and no darkness without the light. I thank the one with long black hair and smiling eyes who is always quietly with me, silhouetted beautifully against the speckled midnight sky and the silvery shimmering glow of the moon. I thank my people, the Eastern Band of Cherokee. Without the voices of the people, there is no "people"; therefore, what we do, we do for the people and for those yet to come.

I thank Barbara and Gerry Clow, John Nelson, and Barbara Doern Drew, my editors at Bear & Company, for their clarity, diligence, and tireless dedication to preserving the wisdom and beauty of the ages by passing on the teachings so that people may better their own lives as well as the lives of all our brothers and sisters. I thank the illustrators, Debi Duke and Francene Hart, for their sacred gift of putting feeling into image, of bringing beauty to life, and for showing us what is truly important.

Finally, I thank you, the reader, for walking this path of peace alongside me and for allowing these ways into your mind and heart. We are all walking the path together. May we be thankful as we walk on the wind, always remembering to taste the beauty all around us. *Wah doh*.

Preface

There was a little boy who used to get up before sunrise to watch "Casper the Friendly Ghost" on a small TV set and eat a snack in the darkness and solitude of the early morning. He would sit there on the carpeted floor, propped against the wall, wondering why no one else wanted to get up with him to watch television or see the sun rise, but he never felt lonely. He loved that quiet time to sit there alone in his flannel pajamas, to think about things and just *be*. He used to sit there and wonder about all kinds of things, just thinking about life—all of the things that were beautiful to him and all of the things that he wanted to create. And sometimes he would think of important questions to ask his mommy and daddy, as well as other special people. Then he would brush his teeth, get dressed, put on his little burgundy low-top Converse "Chucks" (which contained special powers), and go outside into the woods, losing himself in the beauty of Creation where everything has voice, and shape, and color, and feel. Everything moves, everything breathes.

That little boy speaks through me. I am an Eastern Band of Cherokee who bridges worlds. I am neither this nor that. I am both this and that. And in the end, I am as you are—human and spirit. When I speak, although the voices of my people speak through me, I can speak only for myself. I speak from my experiences, my joys and sadness, my limited understanding of this journey we call "life." But most importantly, I speak from the heart. I am hoping that this is what you will hear as you listen to my words, listen to my spirit.

I am a teacher and a student. We are all teachers, and we

are all students. I have learned much about the Medicine from my father and other teachers, just as my father, in turn, learned the Medicine from his grandfather and other medicine teachers. The Medicine is essence. It is all those things that have power for us. It is not easily understood, and yet it flows through us like a chill running down our spine when things suddenly come clear or the calm feeling of listening to the sound of raindrops softly pattering on leaves on a cool rainy day. The Medicine is not about me, and it is not about you; it is about *us*, and it is about life. The Medicine is a way of life. It is a gift. It is a feeling, an inner power that flows through us, guiding us and challenging us to learn so that we can be better helpers to ourselves, all our brothers and sisters around us, and our natural environment.

For all those who seek the truths that lie in our heart of hearts, let us spread our wings and taste the wind. *Walking on the Wind* follows in the footsteps of *Medicine of the Cherokee,* which I coauthored in 1996 with my father, J.T. Garrett, by offering a vision of harmony and balance within oneself and between oneself and all one's "relations" in the Greater Universal Circle. It challenges each of us to look deeper and learn to become a helper in whatever way best expresses our own special Medicine, gifts, and purpose. This is the gift and responsibility of what we know as life. And healing in the traditional Medicine Way occurs *in relation to* people, places, and things.

Although some quotes, stories, and traditions represented in this work come from other tribes, showing the commonality of reverence for the Medicine across tribes and geographic regions, I speak mainly from a Cherokee perspective. Many of the stories and traditional ways described herein are presented as told to me by my father and other elders and teachers. Some of the stories are related as they have been told since the beginning of time, some of the stories are related as I like to tell them, but all in all, the teachings remind us of our humanity and offer us one pathway among many for seeking our own truths.

These ways represent generations of tradition passed down for the good of the people. Many of the teachings presented in this book represent a way of life, a way of spirit, and as I share these things, my hope is to honor my people and remind us all to live with a sense of reverence for the beauty of all life.

Cherokee Sounds

PRONUNCIATION GUIDE

Letter	Sound	Example
a	as *a* in "father" or short as *a* in "rival"	*ama* (water)
e	as *a* in "hate" or short as *e* in "met"	*selu* (corn)
i	as *i* in "pique" or short as *i* in "pit"	*awi* (deer)
o	as *aw* in "law" or short as *o* in "not"	*yonv* (bear)
u	as *oo* in "fool" or short as *u* in "pull"	*uwohali* (eagle)
v	as *u* in "but" (nasalized)	*vdali* (lake)
g	as in English, but with a slight sound of *k*	*gogv* (crow)
d	as in English, but with a slight sound of *l*	*digadoli* (eyes)
h, j, k, l, m, n, q, s, t, w, y		as in English

WALKING
ON THE
WIND

Giving Thanks

O Great One,
We come before you in a humble manner,
Offering what gifts we have,
Giving thanks for the gift of life that we have been given
Amidst the beauty of this Great Creation,
So that we may learn to walk the path of Good Medicine
as we give thanks to each of the Four Directions:
To the spirit of Fire/Sun (warmth and light) in the East,
To the spirit of Earth (peace and renewal) in the South,
To the spirit of Water (purity and strength) in the West,
To the spirit of Wind (wisdom and giving) in the North.
We give thanks to Mother Earth and to the Sacred Fire,
Which burns brightly in our hearts,
Offering us the precious gifts
Of clarity, openness, strength, and wisdom
As we walk the path of peace.
We give thanks to all our relations
And for the beauty of all things,
For those who walk alongside us,
For those who have come before,
And for those yet to come.
In harmony and balance,
We give thanks,
O Great One,
We give thanks.
Wah doh.

Lighting The Fire

As we approach the center, we look around and notice the Circle calmly, peacefully there with us. We watch the passing of the sun and the passing of the moon, one and the same, the Circle of Life that never ends. We feel our footsteps moving lightly upon the ground, and we feel Mother Earth breathing quietly, touching us silently.

We enter the Circle with a reverence for all the beauty that exists around us. We notice the smell of sage and tobacco, sweetgrass and cedar, and we feel the sacredness of the moment—always that moment forever. We notice the smell of the soil beneath us and we see the flowers and trees and little plants that fill our head with the many colors of the rainbow—one light from end to end, from beginning to beginning. We enter the Circle, and we bring with us all those things that have power for us, all of the feelings, all of the memories, all of the people we have known and know now, all of the places, the faces, and the experiences that have brought us to this moment.

Each of the seven sacred woods is laid upon the center, one after the other, with prayers offered in thankfulness and humility. We can smell the distinct aroma of each piece of wood as it offers itself in splendor and the wisdom of time. We can feel the rhythm of the drum penetrating our body and mind, vibrating and whispering to our spirit in an ageless river flowing through all that is. And with each heartbeat of the drum, we can hear the distant footsteps of our ancestors and those yet to come. Like the gentle rain, they are always there, always moving calmly in the soft, misty light of the dim early morning and quiet evening's fall. We see them moving slowly, shifting in unison, smiling in the distance.

Again the prayers are offered, and we can feel the warmth upon our skin as the Sacred Fire is lighted. We inhale, we exhale; inhale and exhale. This is our breath of life. These are our sacred words offered in the timeless beauty of the Circle of Life. We are flowing as sunlight upon Mother Earth; we are flowing as greenery slowly offering life and rising; we are flowing as the river's ancient song; we are flowing as the wind's whispering voice.

Upon the fire, sacred tobacco is sprinkled and begins its journey to the Creator, conveying the thoughts and feelings of those in the Circle. The prayers tell of the way in which we come before the Creator in a humble manner giving thanks for the beauty of Creation, and through the wood and ashes of the fire, we again see our connection with Mother Earth. Through the billowing smoke that rises, faintly twisting into the Sky World, we see our connection with the Creator and all that is. As we watch the smoke dance on the wind in harmony and balance, we remember what it is like to move upon the wind—boundless, limitless, and flowing through all that is. Let the fire be lighted.

CHAPTER ONE

Sun and Moon

*Love is something you and I must have. We must
have it because our spirit feeds upon it. We must have
it because without it we become weak and faint. . . .
Without it our courage fails. Without love, we can no
longer look confidently at the world. We turn inward
. . . and little by little we destroy ourselves. With it,
we are creative. With it, we march tirelessly. With it,
and with it alone, we are able to sacrifice for others.*
—CHIEF DAN GEORGE, COAST SALISH

And so it goes that long before Elohino, Mother
Earth, was old and wise as she is now, there was a
young man named Iga-e-hinvdo, Sun, who lived in
the east, while in the distant west lived a young woman
named Udosvno-e-hi, Moon. Sun was revered by all as the
Creator's young apprentice and as a fearless traveler who
walked the sky searching for a magic lake that was said to

have great healing powers. It was said that when the Creator shaped the world, upon standing back and seeing the beauty that had been made, the Great One was so moved that teardrops began to fall from the Creator's eyes, forming the magic lake on that very spot. This was a sacred place of healing and comfort for those in need, and it allowed one's spirit to see clearly things as they truly are. It was said that to seek out the waters of this magic lake and look upon your own reflection in its rippling surface was to receive your vision and come into the Medicine.

Even as a young man, Sun intended to become a medicine man, who would offer himself as a helper to those in need. He knew that in order to be a part of the Medicine, one had to walk in harmony and balance, moving higher than Uwohali, Eagle, and lower than Ujiya, Worm. But Sun, who was still young and curious, often wandered the sky appreciating all of the beautiful things there were to see and sometimes forgetting his "purpose." He was happy to be alive. During the days, he would walk on the wind, watching all of the lush greenery falling away beneath his footsteps as he moved, looking for the magic lake and the power held in its deep waters. There was such beauty in this journey of life and so much to learn. During the nights, he spent time in his medicine lodge sweating and praying, singing and listening to the silence of the darkness to know what the Great One intended for him.

Moon was a beautiful young woman who seemed to glow in the dim light of the west and become brighter as the darkness grew. She was respected by all of her relations for her kindness, compassion, and gentleness. She moved calmly and peacefully, always offering her comforting presence to those around her, though she was desperately shy. Moon had a great love for Sun and secretly wished to be with him. She admired him from a distance, but retreated whenever he was around. He was like no other man she had ever known, and his presence made her tingle all over. Sun never paid much attention to her, though. He always seemed to be too busy searching for his Medicine to notice the quiet, unassuming young woman who loved him so.

Sun had a lover who used to come to him every month in the dark time of the moon. Since this darkness was supposed to be a sacred time for prayer and reflection, they used to meet in secrecy. She would come to him during the night and leave before daybreak. Together, they would spend much time talking, being close, and sharing beneath the starry sky and velvet darkness. But Sun could never see his lover's face in the darkness, and she would not tell him what her name was. Soon he had fallen deeply in love with this silent woman who made him feel like no one else could. He always got very excited each month when he knew they would be together, and he longed for her painfully when they were apart.

Eventually Sun's curiosity about his secret lover's identity grew, and he devised a plan to find out who she was. So came the time once again when Sun sat quietly in prayer in the sacred darkness just beyond the horizon of the sky and his secret lover came to him gently, excitedly, as she always did. And as they were sitting together, Sun reached into the ashes of the firepit and rubbed some of the blackness on her face without her knowing it, saying, "Your face is cold . . . you must have suffered from the wind." Time passed quickly that evening, and before long, she slipped quietly away once again as she always did.

The next night, when Moon came up in the sky, Sun was watching intently from his hiding place behind the horizon. He peeked through the arch of a shimmering rainbow as it faded, searching the sky for some sign of the one who had been coming to him. Suddenly, he noticed that Moon's face was covered with ashy spots, and he realized that it was Moon who was his secret lover. As he jumped out from his hiding place, Moon knew that she had been found out. Embarrassed, Moon went as far away from Sun as she could and stayed on the other side of the sky all night.

Ever since that time, Moon always tries to stay a long way behind Sun. And when she sometimes has to come close to him, she makes herself as thin as a ribbon so that she can hardly be seen. And yet, out of her deep love for Sun and in remembrance of the time when he touched her for an instant, she has never wiped away the ashy spots that he left upon her glowing face. If you look close enough, you can still see them. And some people say that the stars are glittering teardrops that trickle down Moon's face and fall into the sky when she is missing Sun.

Each day, high in the sky, Sun still searches for his vision and for his lover, Moon, who always seems to be just on the other side of the horizon. And so, it is good.

CHAPTER TWO

The Rule of Acceptance

When you arise in the morning, give thanks for the morning light, for your life and strength. Give thanks for your food and the joy of living. If you see no reason for giving thanks, the fault lies in yourself.
—TECUMSEH, SHAWNEE

There were many things that fascinated me as a child, like the story of Sun and Moon. It helped me to understand why things were the way they were, but, most importantly, that there is value in everything beyond what we may see as opposites, such as good or bad, happy or sad, right or wrong, love or hate. I began to see that there is beauty and simplicity in everything, and I learned how to look beyond the limitations of my own perception. I began to feel the importance of harmony and balance as a way of life.

Therefore, stories like these helped me learn that everything has a place, a time, and a purpose for being—something my father taught me was known as the "Rule of Acceptance." My job, as I understood it, was to discover through the stories what beauty something might hold for me and what truth something has in and of itself. That was the way to understanding harmony and balance—by looking for the beauty and lessons that are offered to us in every experience.

In the traditional way, there is no one moral to a story. The power of it lies in the listener's subjective experience of the story. Whatever lessons are most needed at the time emerge for the person as the spirit seeks to grow. As the elders would say, "You have to sit with it. . . ." Something like the love between Sun and Moon, for example, can be better understood as the natural harmony and balance that is needed in order for us to survive. It is an energy that exists in and of itself. It is just because it is.

Even at a young age, I began to intuitively understand the simplicity and power of such traditional teachings. I also still saw only what was on the surface sometimes. Little did I know that one of my most important lessons was yet to come.

When I was about ten years old, my family and I went out to eat at a family-owned restaurant, in Asheville, North Carolina, that was operated by a Greek man known for his kindheartedness, friendliness, warmth, and, of course, good food. He would come around to each table during the meal, asking how everyone was doing, how they were enjoying the meal, and just making friendly conversation. He loved children and gave candy to them whenever they were at his restaurant because he liked to see them smile.

As a child, I had a real taste for candy, particularly sour candy and Butterfinger candy bars. After this meal, we went to the front counter to pay, and I asked if I could have a Butterfinger. The Greek man, overhearing my request, reached behind the counter and happily handed me a Chick-O-Stick. He did not have any Butterfingers, so he was offering me what he did have—as a gift. Now, for those who do not come from Chick-O-Stick country, you have to understand that it has the same crunchy peanut butter inside that a Butterfinger has, but instead of having a chocolate coating, the Chick-O-Stick has a coating of shredded coconut. Sounds yummy, right?

Well, as a boy, there were many things in the world that I had not yet experienced. Chick-O-Stick was one of those things. The package shows a picture of a chicken. So, naturally, I assumed that it was made out of chicken and tasted like chicken. The thought of a chicken-tasting candy bar somehow did not fit my expectation of an after-dinner treat, and I thought this man must be crazy. And there he was beaming at me, offering me this "chicken bar." Cringing at the thought of eating a chicken candy bar, I refused his gift, saying, "I don't want it." My parents' faces were frozen stiff with horror and disbelief at my behavior. I had just rejected an unselfish offer and insulted a good man. I did not get a Butterfinger that day. And I did not get a Chick-O-Stick either.

What I got was a good long "talking to" about how we Garretts do not act like that, about how important it is to be gracious and respectful and appreciative of things that come our way. I also got sentenced to a month with no candy whatsoever and no chance for probation. Before long, I was going through severe withdrawal effects, with a desperate inner craving for the taste of sweetness to once again grace my mouth and fill my tummy.

That was the longest month of my life. It was also very enlightening. Sometimes we do not have a true sense of appreciation for something until we no longer have it. And it helps us see things in a totally different light.

I remember thinking of candy often during that month, watching as others devoured it, while I could not. I developed a new appreciation for candy and the truly spiritual experience of eating it. At the same time, fruit of all kinds and graham crackers spread with peanut butter became my best friends. But more than that, I learned how important it is to look beyond the surface and the immediate experience, and to always carry oneself in a humble manner. In my four weeks of solitary confinement from candy, I was transformed into one who would never look at the world the same again. Now, there is no way that I could have known that Chick-O-Sticks are not made out of chicken, but, nonetheless, that was not the point. I had hurt the Greek man's feelings.

You can probably think of many things in your own life that you regret, things that you wish you could take back, things that you wish you could go back and do over again. Yet I learned much from that experience that is such an integral part of who I am as a person today. I cannot go back and undo the threads of the past, and I would not want to. I have a saying that I have shared with many people: "The past is the past. Let it be." The self-destruction that occurs through guilt or blame takes one out of harmony and balance, though these things, too, offer important lessons.

However, once something is done, it is done. And all you can do is the best you can do at that point in time given what you have available to you. So once something has happened, all you can do is the best you can do from that point on, which also may mean having an opportunity to correct or compensate for, as is the traditional Cherokee Way, wrongs committed in order to restore the balance and peace. This does not mean forgetting what has happened, but it does mean doing whatever needs to be done in order to let go of harmful energies or emotions such as anger, jealousy, resentment, and guilt so as not to become burdened or blind to the natural flow of life and our own purpose in this flow or Greater Circle, Donelawega.

The past is the past. And yet, regardless, it is also very much alive in our hearts. It is very much a part of who we are. For who are we but the culmination of all of our experiences and memories and perceptions? The spirit is an inner record of all of our experiences, good and bad, positive and hurtful. Who are we but the choices that we make right now at this very moment—the way that we see things and how we respond to everything that happens around us and within us?

Candy has never tasted the same to me, and although I might wish that I had acted differently, I am grateful for the way that it did happen because that experience taught me more by the way that it occurred than if it had never occurred at all. This is one of the many lessons of the Rule of Acceptance: how to make sense out of things that we experience in life, see beauty in these things, and be at peace with them (even if they are painful).

I have many memories of my past, and there are also many things that I do not recollect or that seem fuzzy in my mind. There are many experiences that I remember one way, while others who were also there remember them another way. And many of my memories have changed as I have changed. That is because as I change, I see them in a different light. And so these experiences that are so much a part of me continue to offer me many lessons long after the experience has occurred. These are my truths. And you have your own truths.

When you think back over your own life to this point, what do you see? Do you see missed opportunities? Do you see pain, joy, hardship, luck? What do you see when you look in the mirror? Do you see "wish I could, wish I was . . ." or do you see "glad I did, glad I am . . ."? It is not easy to take a good look at where we are in our lives, particularly since we have so many things to which to pay attention.

When I think back over my life to this point, I remember many faces, many places, many things happening to me, and many of my choices that have carried me to where I am now and where I may be someday. I remember things like Chick-O-Sticks being offered to me unselfishly in the place of Butterfingers, and I remember looking up at the moon in the darkness of the evening, squinting to see the ashy spots on her beautiful pale face. I remember stories, and I remember all of those people who have contributed in some way to who I am today. And I am grateful. Maybe we all are searching for the magic lake in our own way. Maybe we have glimpsed it and didn't realize it. Maybe its reflection shines in every living being. This is the continuing process of life in which we are invited to learn and grow and shine brighter than before.

I remember being very curious as a child. I asked many inquisitive, thought-provoking questions and took many nice toys apart because I wanted to see what they looked like on the inside (much to the dismay of my family). Everything seemed to hold a mysterious secret, and I was bound and determined to unlock these secrets—just because they were there. For all those who are parents or who work with small children, you know that the main purpose of our little ones is to teach us things that we have forgotten, and I did just that. While many adults await the dreaded question from children "Where do babies come from?" I asked no such thing, being too interested in all the other things that there were to learn about in the world. I can remember asking things like:

"Why is the sky blue?"
"Where does the sun come from?"
"Why do birds fly?"
"How does the moon stay in the sky?"
"Why doesn't Melissa [my sister] have a penis?"
"What's at the end of a rainbow?"
"Why are buildings square?"
"Do plants breathe like we do?"

To me, these were important questions deserving important answers.

Now when a child asks you questions like these, there are many approaches you can take. One approach is the scientific approach, in which you can attempt to explain things in a logical, rational, sequential manner, hoping not to overwhelm the child with too much information or information that will only complicate things (or make you uncomfortable). This approach (and all others), of course, inevitably leads to the child's natural follow-up question, "Why?" which leads in turn to the child's next natural follow-up question, "Why?" and so on and so forth.

Another approach is the magical approach, in which,

drawing upon the natural ability and tendency of a child to be creative and imaginative, one tries to explain things in terms that will be easily accepted by the little one given his or her current view of the world (after all, storks really do deliver babies). Yet another very popular approach is diversion, in which one quickly responds by saying, "Go ask your mother" or "Go ask your father" or some other convenient scapegoat.

There is another approach, less popular and not quite as effective, called the honest approach, in which one simply says, "I don't know," but this one is not often used because adults can be too proud to admit that they don't really know or they may assume that they really *do* know. And there are many other approaches used for fielding children's inquiries.

My parents used a combination of approaches in fielding my questions, but the approach that I recall most clearly was the one used most often by my father, called the "Rule of Acceptance." To this day, there are many instances in which he will resort to this approach with me and others. The way it would work is like this:

> *Me:* "How does the crystal work?"
> *Him:* "Well, that's the Rule of Acceptance." (End of conversation.)
> *Me:* "Yeah, but why . . . ?" (To no avail.)
> *Him:* "You will understand when it is time for you to understand."

Now, I am not saying that this was always the way he responded to my questions, or you might start thinking that he was not very helpful. Of course, at the time, I remember thinking that in fact he either did not know the answer or did not want to tell me. In my perception, the Rule of

Acceptance seemed like an easy out for him. After all, it takes a great deal of time and patience to explain something to a child. But I came to understand that the Rule of Acceptance is much more than an easy out, and it is a very basic part of the Cherokee Way.

There are many instances in which the Rule of Acceptance left me frustrated and unfulfilled in my quest for knowledge, and so, determined to satisfy myself, I went in search of the answers I required. Looking back on several times when I received the Rule of Acceptance in response to my questions, I can understand the wisdom of its implementation. There are many things about which I have inquired that if given an answer, I never would have had to seek my own answer and, therefore, might never have truly understood. There are also many instances in which if told "the answer," I would not have accepted it anyway. The point here is not the knowledge, or even necessarily how I received the knowledge, but whether or not I was ready for the answer. This is another important lesson of the Rule of Acceptance: Sometimes it is not the right answer that is important, but asking the right question and being ready for whatever comes.

Part of what has made my father such a good father is that he has had the ability to recognize when my spirit was ready and when it was not. To me, that is the mark of a good teacher. One cannot teach algebra to students who have not yet mastered their multiplication tables or who do not want to learn algebra. One cannot teach advanced literature to students who have not yet mastered the ability to read. And one cannot teach a bird how to fly when its wing feathers have not fully grown in, its eyes are not yet sharp enough to avoid collisions, and its balance is not yet fully developed. Everything is a process that is often gradual and builds upon itself. This process often also requires openness, diligence, and patience, with a little bit of time mixed in.

And so, thanks to the Rule of Acceptance, I learned many things in a proper sequence, learned when and if I was truly ready (and open to learning it), and, in some instances, learned things the hard way. Regardless, my understanding of things, albeit incomplete and forever changing, is my own. Sometimes, only *we* can teach ourselves best what we most need to learn. And I continue to learn more every day I am alive.

Many people have asked me if I am a student (because I look so young), to which I reply, "Yes, aren't we all?" I am a student of life; I will always be a student of life, as are all of us. And sometimes it is not as important to know *why* as it is to know *what*. It is the difference between *knowing* and *feeling*. It is the difference between spending energy—trying to "figure things out"—and making ourselves available to the natural flow of energies around us and to our own unique place within them. And so I learned about the Medicine, much like my father did, much like my grandmother did, much like my great-grandfather did, and so on, by observing and listening, and not necessarily by asking questions. After all, as my father put it, "If you have to ask, you're not ready anyway."

Things that need to happen have a way of happening regardless of how we think they should happen, regardless of how we think they should be, regardless of what we *expect*. Therefore, our greatest responsibility sometimes is to let things unfold naturally and make good choices as we go, rather than forcing things to happen. That is not to say "do nothing," but rather do things wisely—and all in good time.

Understanding the flow of life allows us to let go of expectations, accept the limitations over which we have no control, and move with this flow. This way, we focus our "Nuwati" (energies) on making intuitively informed choices about where our path is taking us and learn from the beauty of life—allowing our own spirit to flourish like a small wildflower opening its dewy petals to the bright and orangey morning sunlight. Expect nothing and appreciate the value of everything; this is the true lesson of the Rule of Acceptance. There is a passage in *I Heard the Owl Call My Name*, by Native American novelist Margaret Craven, that reminds me of the Rule of Acceptance:

> I think it is time you knew of Tagoona, the Inuit. Last year one of our white men said to him, "We are glad you have been ordained as the first priest of your people. Now you can help us with their problem." Tagoona asked, "What is a problem?" and the white man said, "Tagoona, if I held you by your heels from a third-story window, you would have a problem." Tagoona considered this long and carefully. Then he said, "I do not think so. If you saved me, all would be well. If you dropped me, nothing would matter. It is you who would have the problem." (p. 74)

My father was learning from his grandfather once, and he kept saying "I think" this and "I think" that. . . . Finally his grandfather said very calmly but firmly, "I think maybe you should stop thinking so much and listen. . . ." The danger in thinking that we know everything is that we then forget to listen and be intentional in making ourselves available to the continuous flow of life experiences and learning that comes to us, sometimes in the simplest of ways.

There is an old Cherokee saying: "Listen, or your tongue will make you deaf!" The Rule of Acceptance teaches us about the importance of listening and opening up our spirits by giving away the *need to control* or change other people, the *need to control* things, or the *need to control* situations. These things remove us from the harmony and balance of the Circle, and just make life difficult when it does not have to be. Life is long (enough); relax and enjoy living it. And then you, too, can use the Rule of Acceptance on someone else.

P.S. If you have never eaten a Chick-O-Stick, I would highly recommend that you do so some time in your life. The dentist would say that it is not good for your teeth, but you never know what you might learn from something so simple . . .

Francene Hart '93

CHAPTER THREE

Clearing the Muddied Waters

What is life? It is the flash of a firefly in the
night. It is the breath of a buffalo in the winter
time. It is the little shadow which runs across the
grass and loses itself in the Sunset.
—CROWFOOT, BLACKFOOT, 1890 (ON HIS DEATHBED)

It is my opinion that we have become dependent upon technology to live our lives. This, in itself, is neither bad nor good; modern technology serves a purpose. It is simply one way of doing things, among many ways of doing things. It is one truth among many truths. But in our search for newer and better technology, is it possible that we have forgotten how to depend on our own *internal* technology, that which provides us with everything we ever need to know in order to live and learn and grow? Could it be that we have allowed our sacred stream of consciousness to become muddied with facts and figures and the need for life to be quick and easy? In creating technology to "simplify" our lives, might we have also further complicated them? In today's world of information and speed, it is important not to forget why we are here. Life has a way of reminding us when we listen.

....

LISTENING TO YOUR
"CELLULAR PHONE"

Have you ever been thinking of someone in particular—maybe a close friend with whom you haven't spoken in a long time—when all of a sudden the phone rings, and it's that person? And you say to your friend, "Wow! I was just thinking about you; that's really strange that you called me right now." And your friend says, "Well, I just had this funny urge to call you." The connection is made.

Or have you ever had the similar experience of having someone whom you haven't seen in awhile just keep coming to your mind, and the next thing you know, you happen to bump into him or her totally unexpectedly? And you say, "You know, you've kind of been on my mind lately—I've been thinking about old times—and it's really great to see you again." The connection is made.

Have you ever been in a particular place, and you have a sense of familiarity or comfort being there, not just because of the surroundings, but because of the feeling that it gives you? The connection is made.

Have you had the experience of being somewhere when all of sudden it is as though something clicks and everything seems familiar, while you are left with the eerie feeling that whatever just happened has happened before? And that familiar feeling lingers with you for a time and then slowly fades? It is the same feeling as that of having a dream that seemed *so* real to you while you were there—every sight, sound, feeling, face, shape, place, flow of events—that you would swear you were just there or that it had just happened. And that feeling lingers with you for some time until eventually it begins to fade, becoming distant and hard to remember. Thus, the connection is made for a time.

How do you explain the feeling of connectedness and familiarity that these situations evoke or the power of that feeling that may last for seconds, or days, or a lifetime? Is it the past or the present or *you* becoming consciously aware of something that is there anyway?

If you have ever had any of these situations happen to you, then you were probably listening to your inner "cellular phone." I say that in somewhat of a joking manner, and yet it is said with much truth. If you consider that every cell of your body contains all of the memory of everything you have ever experienced through time, then you have trillions and trillions of minute cellular phones all connected by the energy that makes you alive and fully functioning to ensure your survival, well-being, and ability to adapt.

Our awareness (or lack of awareness) of all this memory, however, presents us with challenges whereby, in order to understand, we must overcome our own limited perceptions of time and space. What we use in spirit to understand our world is our mind. Researchers have suggested that our consciousness can be characterized by four different levels of activity:

1. *Beta.* This is the level of consciousness in which we function for about sixteen hours per day. About 75 percent of beta regulates our life-controlling bodily

functions such as heartbeat, breathing, digestion, while the other 25 percent is left to deal with our conscious thoughts.

2. *Alpha*. This is what many have referred to as the subconscious mind, entered into by such activities as meditation, biofeedback, and daydreaming, among others. Alpha has a 95 to 100 percent concentration efficiency, which is superior to the 25 percent efficiency of the "conscious," or beta, level, and it is not the same as being asleep.

3. *Theta*. This is the part of the unconscious mind that functions in light sleep. "Unconscious" is used to refer to being unawake and unaware; this is not the same as "subconscious," referring to a different state of wakefulness and awareness.

4. *Delta*. This is the level of deep sleep in which the unconscious mind obtains the greatest amount of rest. This level of mental activity lasts for a total of about thirty or forty minutes each night.

These four levels of mental activity occur in sequence, moving from full consciousness (beta) to a subconscious state (alpha) to light sleep (theta) to deep sleep (delta) and in reverse through the same sequence for awakening. Thus, the mind moves through a natural cycle that allows us to function at an optimal level and heal when we need to heal. In addition, the cycle affects and is affected by such factors as stress, nutrition, medication/substance use, and exercise/physical fitness, all of which determine how well we function by contributing to or disrupting our own harmony and balance. Both our mental and physical dimensions are dependent on this cycle of consciousness for survival. However, this cycle provides us with more than survival—it provides us with an opportunity to tap a level of awareness that transcends the mental and physical dimensions.

Alpha is the level of mental activity in which we are most receptive to messages through our cellular phone, given a state of calm and relaxation that allows things to flow. But there are other times when important messages reach us even when we are in beta, or a state of full consciousness. Beta is a state of mind that allows us to think through and understand on a cognitive level what it is that we are experiencing or have experienced.

Sometimes we pick up our cellular phone unintentionally, through dreaming, déjà vu, or feelings that just come over us, and maybe it catches us a little off guard. Sometimes, through such things as meditation, prayer, relaxation, pursuing creative endeavors, or connecting with nature, we use our cellular phone quite intentionally. Our spirit has a way of moving, whether *we* are meaning to or not. That is one of the good things about sleep: it not only rejuvenates our physical self, but it also rejuvenates and clears our mind so that we are ready to receive whatever is next. It gives our mind and spirit a chance to work together to clear whatever has been in our thoughts lately and to teach us deeper lessons to which we do not always make ourselves readily available in our waking hours.

Our spirit is like a bird that knows only that it is supposed to fly. A bird does not think about why it is supposed to fly, or how, or when—it just does it. Although there are birds who haven't flown in so long that they have forgotten how to fly or even what it feels like to walk upon the wind. And there are birds that are still growing their wings although they have not yet tasted the wind.

The way that the spirit moves is by experiencing and learning, and every cell in our body is a living record of all that has gone before. Interestingly, all of the cells in our body go through a gradual process of renewal and replacement so that about every nine months, all of the cells in our body have been replaced by new cells. Yet even though the physical structure changes and eventually has to be renewed or replaced, the memory is preserved as it is passed on from one cell to another through the continuing process of life and regeneration.

So when we use our cellular phone (which, coincidentally, is much less expensive than the plastic ones created through modern technology), we are tapping a connection with all our relations, the energy of Mother Earth, and the universe itself in an ancient and very sacred network of life energy, or Nuwati. It is quite handy, actually. We don't need a calling card. There are no monthly bills or extra charges. There is no limit to the number of calls, length of calls, or range of our cellular phone. And we can use it for several purposes: We can call ourselves, we can call others, we can call our surroundings, we can call through time. It is unlimited and very, very useful. What's more, it is built into our physical being. There is only one catch: We have to learn how to use it and to do so responsibly.

....

PICKING UP THE RECEIVER

The first step is learning how to pick up your cellular phone. Obviously, this is much harder to do while in a state of full consciousness because our brain can get in the way.

Therefore, it is important to pay attention to certain feelings of intuition (not the same as "opinions") that you may have about yourself, others, or your surroundings. It is also important to seek places that will allow you to enter a state of calm without distraction or interference. This might mean seeking out or creating a safe place in which you can tap your cellular phone and seek your visions, which simply means learning to listen. A conducive place is one that *feels* particularly good to you or has good energy for you. Then, let your mind be still.

• •

MAKING THE CONNECTION

The second step is learning how to make the connection. This is where listening, patience, and openness are critical. Do not rush anything or force anything or try too hard. This is a matter of opening up and letting go of expectations, distractions, insecurities, fears. Here, it is important to be aware of self-imposed limits or restrictions such as fears, insecurities, and rigid beliefs, which interfere with or block our ability to perceive and receive. Fear really is our worst enemy, though sometimes our best teacher. Of course, the best way of facing fear is by embracing it and *doing* whatever it is that we most fear. Opening up is a gradual process and occurs naturally when we learn to make ourselves available to the process, to trust the process, and to make ourselves available to the flow of Nuwati.

A good place to start is by placing your fingers on your pulse and paying attention to only your pulse—the way it feels against your fingertips, how fast it is moving, and how strong. Once you learn to pay attention to your heart *literally*, it is much easier to pay attention to your heart *figuratively*.

··

SEEING WHAT'S THERE

The third step is learning to recognize the connection once we have made it. There is a big difference between *knowing* something and *feeling* something. As Phil Lane, Yankton Lakota elder, put it in *Native Wisdom for White Minds* by Anne Wilson Schaef, (July 25), "For every problem solved by the mind, it creates ten more . . . we need to get to the heart or soul!" This is probably one of the biggest keys to knowing when you have made the connection: You are left with a different sense about things, and it is something that you *feel*, as well as *know*. Do not fall into the trap of trying to interpret things—just let them come to you and make sense of them later.

If you are choosing to use your sleep time as a way of using your cellular phone, you may want to give yourself the following suggestion quietly in your own mind both before you go to bed and as you are drifting off: "I will remember when I wake up whatever is important for me to remember." This helps your mind to focus and to remember much more effectively. It may also be particularly helpful to keep a journal (filled with pictures, stories, descriptions of images or events, etc.) of things that come to you in your dreams.

Then, the only other thing is to pay attention to what comes to you in the form of images, particular words or phrases, and certain feelings. Taken together, these images, words, and feelings may not seem to make sense at first, but given some time, things will often begin to fall into place, making much more sense as you step back from them. It is much like putting together a puzzle. You are able to look at each individual piece and look at all of the pieces individually lying together before you. Then, as you step back, the picture begins to take shape in front of you with all of the pieces coming together (even the ones that didn't seem to fit anywhere).

As images, words, and feelings are coming to you, become as sensual as you can. Notice landscape or scenery (with any distinguishing characteristics), what the climate is like, particular noises or smells, whether there is anyone else around or if you are alone, what you are doing, how you are feeling, what you are thinking, and any other details or impressions that stand out for you.

··

KNOWING WHAT TO DO WITH IT

The fourth step is learning what to do with the connection once it has been made. Developing your ability to "sense things" means that you therefore must also make a choice about what to do with the things that come to you. There is no hard and fast rule here, but consider the following questions:

- Are you in a position of being a helper to someone or something?
- If so, what would be the consequences of your influencing a person or situation?
- Does the person or situation *want* to be helped?
- What need, if any, is being met for you by being a helper or by influencing a person or situation (in other words, what do you stand to gain)?

In the Cherokee Way, when confronted with a difficult decision or with a sense of uncertainty, it is important for the person to sit with it for at least four days before taking any action. One of the most important aspects of knowing what to do with the connection is learning to trust your feeling, or intuitive sense, about things. Your feeling is there for the purpose of offering you important insight into things around you and within you. If you find yourself trying hard to understand things or interpret things, you will discover that not much comes to you (remember the Rule of Acceptance?). It is not so much what you *believe* to be true, but what you *experience* as true that matters in the realm of spirit.

It is not as important to validate and verify what you sense as it is to follow your spirit. Sometimes, people will ask me, "How do you know that?" to which I will often reply, "It's just a feeling I have, that's all. . . . It might be off." The wisest person is the one who is humble enough to admit that he or she may be wrong, knowing that he or she also may not be wrong. Even when we develop our ability to sense things, we still are human and have subjective perceptions or judgments that might interfere with the nature of the message by the way we interpret it.

If you try to use what comes to you in order to control others or interfere with their lessons, then you are taking away from them a very sacred gift that is not yours to take. Then, too, you will find that the flow of images, words, and feelings will stop coming to you. Once again, the purpose of the Medicine is to act as a helper, not to control others or be self-indulgent and self-important. Using the Medicine in a proper way involves respecting what the spirit needs and allowing things to happen in their own time.

Using your cellular phone, therefore, is not a matter of pride or personal opinion. All you can do is the best you can do given what you know or feel at the present moment—and given your continued openness to exploring the way of the spirit. In fact, one of the first lessons of the Medicine is clarity through humility. It is a very sacred experience to make the connection and open yourself to the Nuwati. It is an honor to become the most that anyone can ever hope to become: a helper.

Francene Hart 92

CHAPTER FOUR

Doing What's Natural

*To be a Medicine person, you have to experience
everything, live life to the fullest. If you don't experience the human side of everything, how can you help
teach or heal? To be a good Medicine person, you've
got to be humble. You've got to be lower than a worm
and higher than an eagle.*

—ARCHIE FIRE LAME DEER, LAKOTA MEDICINE MAN

And so it goes that there was a time when all creatures
on Elohino (Mother Earth) lived together in harmony and balance, including human beings. But as
there began to be more and more people, the animals found
themselves getting crowded out. Then people began to make
weapons such as bows and arrows, knives, blowguns, spears,
and hooks in order to kill animals, birds, and fish for their
flesh or skins. And this was alright as long as the people fol-
lowed the natural laws of Creation by respectfully informing

the animals of their intentions, asking permission from the animal spirits, killing only when necessary for survival, using every part of what was received, and always giving thanks by making an offering (of tobacco) to the animal's spirit. But when the people started forgetting these things, and on top of everything else the smaller creatures started getting kicked around, the animals finally decided that things had gone too far and decided to meet in council to choose what must be done.

The first to meet in council were Yonv, the bears. Speaking softly, but with great strength and wisdom, Old White Bear Chief emphasized the importance of what they were about to decide and passed the talking stick so that each had his or her chance to share thoughts about what should be done. After much talk, the bears decided that they would make a bow and arrows such as the one people used against them. So together they fashioned a bear-size bow with arrows, but when they tried to shoot it, they found that their claws kept getting in the way. They found that if they cut their claws, and with a little practice, they could hit their mark. But this left Old White Bear Chief in great dismay, saying, "If we cut our claws, we will starve. It is better to trust our teeth and claws, for this is the traditional way of us bears."

Next to hold council were Awi, the deer. They, too, had much talk about all of the harms committed against them, and many hours passed. Then, through the guidance of their chief, Little Deer, they decided to curse with rheumatism each hunter who did not follow the natural laws of Creation. Word was sent to all of the communities of people about what would happen if they did not follow the natural laws out of reverence for the Greater Circle. Little Deer was so fast that he could not be wounded. He would run to a spot where a deer had been killed and ask, "Did the hunter pray and do things in a proper way?" If the deer spirit answered yes, then Little Deer would go on his way. But if the deer spirit answered no, then Little Deer would follow the trail of the hunter by the drops of blood on the ground, and he would strike the hunter with painful rheumatism.

Atsadi, fish and reptiles, also held their council and decided to make people have nightmares so that they would lose their appetite and die. Walasi, the frog, cried out, "People have kicked me around so much that my back is covered with sores!"

Tsi's-qua, birds, and insects too expressed great outrage in their council over people's cruelty and disregard. Tsi-s-qua exclaimed, "The people pluck out all our feathers, and burn our feet over the barbecue!" The insects said, "They step on us, and then just wipe us off their moccasins as if it were nothing!"

Then all of the animals came together in a large council, and they began to come up with so many diseases that surely all of the people would be wiped out. Little Grubworm was so happy that he fell backward and couldn't get up on his feet again.

When Ahwisga, the plants, caught word of what the animals had done, they were very unhappy. Yes, they too had been stepped on and mistreated by people, but they knew that the way to make things right was not through harmful ways. After all, people needed to have the chance to learn from their mistakes so that they could once again be the helpers and protectors that the Great One intended them to be.

So the plants came together in council to talk about a way to restore the harmony and balance once again. Each tree, shrub, and herb—even the moss and grass—offered to help people in whatever way it could when the people were afflicted with disease. Each one said, "I will always be there to help when people call upon me in their time of need." To this day, any time a medicine man or medicine woman is treating someone, the spirit of the plant tells him or her what to use. And so, it is good.

....

UNDERSTANDING THE NATURAL FLOW

I recall stories like this one about the origin of disease and medicine, and many more, that remind us how crucial it is to understand and contribute to the natural flow by being a "helper" to our relations. I remember once listening to a Mayan elder talk about one day when he was walking in the forest with a young boy who had cut off one of the branches of a small tree. The boy was proud of his new walking stick and displayed it for the elder to see. The elder questioned whether the boy had gone about it in a proper way: asking permission, taking only what he needed, and giving thanks to the tree spirit by making some offering. The boy replied that he had just cut it off because he needed a good walking stick and the branch was a good one for that. The elder asked the boy to go back to the tree and put his hand on the spot where he had cut off the branch.

"What did you feel?" he asked the boy.

"It was wet," said the boy.

"That is because the tree was crying," the elder replied.

Simple lessons such as these are powerful in teaching us

to respect our place in the Circle. It is not often that we stop to think of the far-reaching consequences of simple actions on our part because we cannot always see the cycle moving. Think about one such act, related by environmental scientist Barry Commoner in *The Closing Circle*:

> A dry-cell battery containing mercury is purchased, used to the point of exhaustion, and then "thrown out." But where does it really go? First, it is placed in a container of rubbish: this is collected and taken to an incinerator. Here, the mercury is heated; this produces mercury vapor which is emitted by the incinerator stack, and mercury vapor is toxic. Mercury vapor is carried by the wind, eventually brought to Earth in rain or snow. Entering a mountain lake, let us say, the mercury condenses and sinks to the bottom. Here, it is acted on by bacteria which convert it to methyl mercury. This is soluble and taken up by fish; since it is not metabolized, the mercury accumulates in the organs and flesh of the fish. The fish is caught and eaten by a human being and the mercury becomes deposited in that person's organs, where it might be harmful. And so on. (Jones, *The Ecologist* 18, no. 1, p. 33)

So whatever enters the cycle, of which we are only a part, finds its way back to the beginning point in the end, and so on. Commoner also points out that

> an animal, such as the deer, may depend on plants for food; the plants depend on the action of soil bacteria for their nutrients; the bacteria in turn live on the organic wastes dropped by the animals on the soil. At the same time, the deer is food for the mountain lion. (Jones, *The Ecologist* 18, no. 1, p. 33)

All living things are connected in ways that enable life to continue in a balanced and cyclical manner. Mother Earth provides the cycle for both the substance and form of every living being, as described by Commoner:

> For every organic substance produced by a living organism, there exists, somewhere in nature, an enzyme capable of breaking that substance down. In effect, no organic substance is synthesized unless there is provision for its degradation: recycling is thus enforced. (Jones, *The Ecologist* 18, no. 1, p. 34)

The more that we are able to understand the Circle (cycle) of Life and our place within it, the more we are able to understand ourselves, our purpose, our responsibilities, and our Medicine.

....

BEING A HELPER

In the traditional teachings of the Cherokee and other tribes, spiritual and natural laws govern a person's way of life as a helper to one's relations walking together in the Greater Circle. Although there are more than five hundred different tribes in the United States, speaking more than 150 different languages, there exist certain common, universal beliefs that transcend tribal affiliations and individual life in each of the sovereign nations. In common to many tribes and nations across the United States, both traditionally and historically, are the basic beliefs that we should

1. never take more than we need;
2. give thanks for what we have or what we receive;
3. use all of what we have;
4. "Giveaway" what we do not need.

Thus, Native Americans were among the first conservationists and environmentalists, possessing a deep understanding of the delicate balance of human life with all other life in the natural surroundings, all of which was looked upon as a sacred gift from the Creator, to be treated always with reverence and great care. The traditional way of life was based on a very basic set of principles involving demonstration of respect for oneself, one's relatives, or "relations" (all living creatures), Mother Earth, and those in the spirit world. At the center of all of this for the Cherokee was (and still is) the Sacred Fire, which was our direct connection with the Great One, Ogedoda (or Uhalotega).

The sacred beliefs and traditions are often related through stories that convey what it means to walk the path of "Good Medicine"—being in harmony with the universe and its sacred rhythms—and in the case of the "tricksters" (e.g., Rabbit), what happens if you don't. That is not to say, however, that there is only one right way of doing things and that if you don't follow it you will or must be punished. Quite the contrary, in the traditional way choice is valued as the way to learning and is therefore essential to the Medicine Way—in other words, the way of the spirit, or essence of life. The need to control or limit the experiences of another is thought of as the fulfillment of one's own need for power or the selfish expression of one's own fear and insecurity (Rule of Acceptance: letting go of expectation or destructiveness). In fact, you can accept someone without having to agree with his or her way of doing or seeing things. Right and wrong are considered relative and limiting value terms that potentially rob a person of the opportunity to experience life fully in mind, body, spirit, and natural environment, and thus to learn from his or her experiences.

Each tribe, traditionally, has a proper way of doing things that is specified in ceremonies and tribal teachings. These teachings extend from the natural and spiritual laws of Creation. For example, there is a certain way in which one must make prayers and offerings when hunting, fishing, or gathering plants or minerals for survival or for medicine. In addition, one must explain one's intentions to the spirit of the animal, fish, plant, or mineral, also taking great care to never take more than one needs and to use all of what one takes. In the case of plants, Cherokee tradition specifies that one must take only every fourth plant and leave the other three undisturbed. This is done out of respect for the life and great powers of the plants, so that they, too, may survive, and it is done in a spirit of thankfulness, humility, and kinship.

Traditionally, both accidental and deliberate acts of violation require compensation, rather than blame and punishment, in order to restore harmony and balance. One of the greatest privileges and responsibilities bestowed upon all living beings is living as part of the Circle (family, clan, tribe, etc.). Therefore, one of the worst so-called punishments in the traditional way is shunning. In this, one would no longer be acknowledged as a member of anything, and no energy would be wasted on the person who chooses to not respectfully live according to the natural laws of Creation. Imagine the power of being turned away from your connections. Even with shunning, the purpose is not to punish the person, but to maintain the harmony and balance for all of the others, for whom this is a necessary and important part of living.

An extreme case of tribal justice occurred in the early 1990s when two Tlingit teenagers were convicted of robbery and assault with a deadly weapon. The victim, a pizza delivery man, was severely beaten with a baseball bat and remained hearing impaired due to the incident. The two teenagers were sentenced by tribal court as per Tlingit law, which specified restitution for the victim plus one year's banishment for the offenders.

The Tlingit approach called for both rehabilitation of the criminal and assistance for the victim. Without this, the boys could not be accepted back into their tribe, the victim would not be compensated for harm committed against him (and in the Native American way, against his family as well), and the harmony and balance would be left undone. The Tlingit tribe pledged to build the victim a new house and pay for his medical bills. The two boys, meanwhile, were banished to separate uninhabited islands on Native lands in the Gulf of Alaska for twelve months with only some basic hand tools and enough food for two weeks.

Another example of the importance of restoring harmony and balance was described by Ella Deloria, a Lakota anthropologist, who related an incident in which a young murderer was brought before the victim's community to be sentenced according to the Lakota Way:

> The angry relatives debated the kind of consequence fitting the crime while the wise elder listened. After a good while, he began to speak. Skillfully, he began by going along with them.
>
> "My brothers and cousins, my sons and nephews, we have been caused to weep without shame. . . . No wonder we are enraged, for our pride and honor have been grossly violated. Why shouldn't we go out, then, and give the murderer what he deserves?"

Then after an ominous pause, he suddenly shifted. . . .
"And yet, my Kinsmen, there is a better way!"

Slowly and clearly, he explained the better way. It was
also the hard way, but the only certain way to put out the fire
in their hearts and in the murderer's.

"Each of you bring the thing you prize the most. These
things shall be a token of our intention. We shall give them to
the murderer who has hurt us, and he shall thereby become a
relative in place of him who is gone. And from now on, he
shall be one of us, and our endless concern shall be to regard
him as though he were truly our loved one come back to us."
(Brendtro, Brokenleg, and Van Bockern, *Reclaiming Youth
at Risk*, p. 51)

Similar approaches were taken, traditionally, with such
acts as rape or abuse, which were not tolerated as they were
considered violence not only against the body and mind but
also against the spirit. Compensation had to be made to the
victim and/or the victim's family as specified by tribal ways,
and in extreme cases, the offender was sometimes exiled
from the tribe (one of the worst consequences). Violations
against nature or against those in the spirit world brought
their own set of natural consequences requiring no human
intervention, although restitution for such acts often meant
seeking out a medicine man or medicine woman to help the
person come back into harmony and balance, again through
some form of compensation or reconciliation.

The Medicine Way emphasizes the belief that for every
choice or action, there are certain natural or spiritual consequences that provide any person with learning that is necessary for his or her spirit. These consequences are enforced

not necessarily by people, but by those in the spirit world as a way of protecting the Circle and natural way of things. Many of the social laws that existed for tribes provided a means of survival, as well as a specific way of conducting relations so as to respect the natural and spiritual laws of Creation and to allow the people to live in harmony and balance. These ways provided guidance with the knowledge that there were also certain consequences for violating these natural or spiritual laws. For example, violating the natural way was to invite illness or hardship upon oneself and one's family.

You have probably heard the old adage "What goes around, comes around." This is very much a part of the Medicine Way through the belief that everything we put out into the universe comes back to us in some way, shape, or form. However, this does not necessarily have to be a visible act of some kind. In the Medicine, some of the most powerful acts are the thoughts that roam around in our heads every day. I remember an elder once telling me, "Be clear and conscious in what you think and do. This is Medicine that leaves your body, mind, and spirit, like the heat off of your skin and the breath from your mouth, and the wind will bring it back to you."

THE WIND WILL CARRY IT BACK TO YOU

The need for clarity and conscious intention in our lives, with a renewed sense of reverence for all our relations, has become increasingly apparent as we look at what has been occurring around us and within us. The idea that what goes around comes around has become increasingly apparent in recent times as we have experienced the effects of a natural environment struggling to maintain its delicate balance. We have experienced the continued difficulties related to the greenhouse effect, air pollution, ozone depletion, hazardous waste, acid rain, wildlife disappearance, groundwater pollution, and garbage buildup.

In chapter 2, I made the statement that all you can do is the best you can do at that point in time given what you have available. So are we doing all that we can, the best that we can do, not only for ourselves but for all our relations as well? Are we fulfilling our sacred role on Mother Earth as helpers and protectors of life? These are critically important questions—very timely and worth answering. Part of finding our own Medicine is seeing the Medicine in everything around us as well and seeking harmony and balance in all things. As Chief Dan George, Coast Salish elder, once put it, "If you talk to the animals, they will talk with you, and you will know each other. If you do not talk to them, you will not know them, and what you do not know, you will fear. What one fears, one destroys" (McFadden, *The Little Book of Native American Wisdom*, p. 26).

The greenhouse effect. The greenhouse effect, which normally functions to keep our planet warm by maintaining a certain amount of heat in the atmosphere, has been altered by human activity through the burning of fossil fuels and the destruction of forests. The result is that we have increased the amount of carbon dioxide in the atmosphere by more than 25 percent, which threatens the stability of our environment as a warming trend has continued.

Air pollution. The millions of tons of hydrocarbons and nitrogen oxides that are spewed into the atmosphere each year by motor vehicles and utilities, oil, and chemical plants have resulted in lung damage, damage to trees, and crop losses.

Ozone depletion. The release of chlorofluorocarbons (CFCs—e.g., from aerosol spray cans), halons, and other manmade chemicals into the atmosphere has been destroying our planet's protective shield, the ozone layer, which protects Mother Earth's surface from dangerous solar ultraviolet radiation. The result is clearly seen in more skin cancer and cataracts, depressed immune systems, and a reduction in crop yields and fish populations, as well as other possible effects not yet known.

Hazardous waste. The dumping of millions of tons of hazardous waste from chemically derived products such as plastics, detergents, and aerosols has polluted our ground and water through landfills, drains, and sewer sludge.

Acid rain. The release of sulfur dioxide and nitrogen oxides into the atmosphere by coal-burning electric power plants and by motor vehicles has resulted in acidified rain or snow that falls back to Earth, destroying plant and animal life in streams, damaging forests, and eroding buildings.

Wildlife disappearing. As people move into places that used to be inhabited by only plants and animals, forests are cut down and wetlands, oceans, and prairies are invaded. Numerous species of plants and animals have become endangered or extinct.

Groundwater pollution. Since 97 percent of Earth's water supply is contained in the oceans and 2 percent is frozen, we get our water from the remaining 1 percent contained in rivers, lakes, streams, and groundwater. Leakage of gasoline and other harmful pollutants from underground storage tanks, poorly constructed landfills, and septic systems has polluted the groundwater, as have the runoff of pesticides from fertilized fields and industrial areas and the dumping of contaminating materials down the drain.

Garbage. Although recycling has become more popular in recent years, our landfills continue to be overwhelmed with garbage, polluting the land.

....

HELPING ALL OUR RELATIONS

"Whatever befalls the Earth, befalls the sons and daughters of the Earth. This we know. The Earth does not belong to people; people belong to the Earth. This we know. All things are connected like the blood which unites one family. All things are connected." These words spoken by Chief Seattle, Suwamish/Duwamish, in 1855 (upon surrendering tribal lands to the governor of the Washington Territory), still hold much wisdom for us today.

There are many simple things that we can do as helpers to preserve our home, Mother Earth, and protect all our relations. The following are but a few suggestions offered by the Earth Works Group in *50 Simple Things You Can Do to Save the Earth*:

1. Use less detergent, and use a low-phosphate or phosphate-free detergent to reduce contaminants in lakes and streams.

2. Install a low-flow faucet and shower head aerator to conserve water.

3. Use reusable containers to store food instead of aluminum foil, plastic wrap, or plastic bags.

4. Use cloth rags to wipe up spills instead of paper towels.

5. Turn your water heater down to 130 degrees (hot enough to kill bacteria and still save energy).

6. Make sure your tires are properly inflated, balanced, and rotated (every six to eight thousand miles) in order to improve gas mileage and extend tire life; keep your car/truck tuned up to maintain fuel efficiency.

7. Conserve energy, and use energy-efficient lighting.

8. Don't use aerosol cans containing CFCs in order to protect the atmosphere.

9. Use rechargeable batteries, and recycle alkaline batteries when possible.

10. Request as few bags as possible when shopping.

11. When cutting your lawn, "cut it high and let it lie" in order to allow cuttings to serve as a moisture-retentive mulch and natural fertilizer.

12. Use paper cups and plates instead of polystyrene foam.

13. Avoid buying ivory, tortoiseshell, coral, reptile skins, cat pelts, mahogany or other products from endangered animals or plants.

14. Recycle glass, aluminum, plastic, paper, and metal cans, and reuse or recycle old newspapers.

15. Snip each ring of plastic six-pack holders before disposal (so they do not become a danger to marine life).

16. Plant a tree.

....

REMEMBERING THE CIRCLE

Native peoples view all things as having spiritual energy and importance. All things are connected, all things have life, and all things are worthy of respect and reverence. Spiritual "being" essentially requires only that individuals seek their place in the universe; everything else will follow in good time. Because everything was created with a specific purpose to fulfill, no one should have the power to interfere with or to impose upon others which path is the best to follow.

Cherokee spiritual beliefs focus on the necessity of harmony and balance by emphasizing that

1. everything is alive;
2. everything has purpose;
3. all things are connected;
4. we can embrace the Medicine of all living things as we are all walking together in the Circle.

Central to the Cherokee spiritual tradition is the importance of "relation" as a total way of existing in the world. This power of relation is symbolized by the Circle of Life, represented in the customs, traditions, and artforms of our people. This Circle of Life is believed to consist of spirit, nature, body, and mind, referred to as the Four Winds of Life (or the Four Directions). The Circle thus reflects not only the interrelationship of all living beings, but the natural progression or growth of life itself. Harmony and balance are necessary for the survival of all life, and proper relations can never be emphasized enough in the traditional way.

In Cherokee teachings, every living being possesses an

inner power referred to as "Medicine," or way of life, which connects us to all other living beings through the heart. However, if we fail to respect our relations (with all living beings, the Creator, Mother Earth, ourselves, and the Four Directions) and to keep ourselves in step with the universe, we invite illness by falling out of harmony and balance, much like a dancer failing to move in step with the rhythm of the drum. A person's Medicine is his or her power, and it can be used for creative purposes or destructive purposes—either contributing to or taking away from the Greater Circle of Life. Being in harmony means being "in step with the universe"; being in disharmony means being "out of step with the universe."

When we honor the Circle, we honor all that is, all that has ever been, and all that ever will be. When we remember those who have walked before us, we honor the Circle. We *feel* where we are, and we *feel* where we have come from. Following is an old story about Cherokee history that allows us to know the Circle, and how it is always part of us, both in joyous times and in hardship.

In 1830, many Cherokee people began recognizing the growing United States attitude that the presence of the Cherokee and other southeastern tribes was standing in the way of the country's expansionism and other national interests (i.e., greed for gold and land). Cherokee reaction to this was strong, and it carried with it the intention to unite the people in a concerted effort to achieve peaceful means for reconciliation to maintain the harmony and balance, but also protect that which was home. Chief John Ross exclaimed, "Inclination to move from this land has no abiding place in our hearts, and

when we move, we shall move by the course of nature to sleep
under this ground which the Great Spirit gave to our ancestors,
and which now covers them in their undisturbed repose"
(Hifler, *A Cherokee Feast of Days*, p. 240).

However, in 1838, some fourteen thousand Cherokee
were forcibly removed from their homes in the Smoky
Mountains of North Carolina and parts of Tennessee and
Georgia, in what was known as "The Removal." Thus began
the "Trail of Tears," a thousand-mile journey to Oklahoma
that started in the sleet and swirling snow of a November
morning and ended six months later. During this journey,
more than four thousand people died of famine, illness, and
exhaustion. At one time, Cherokee territory had included
western North Carolina, northwestern South Carolina,
northern Georgia, northern Alabama, most of Tennessee,
Kentucky, part of West Virginia, and southwestern Virginia; it
was reduced to a tiny part of North Carolina.

It has been said that as the people walked, the old
women cried for the people. As their tears fell like drops of
rain, the tears turned to corn beads when they touched the
soil, leaving a sacred trail in the wake of the people's heavy
footsteps. The Cherokee people who reached Oklahoma
began what is today known as the Cherokee Nation. But
once the Indian people were there, the soldiers had no way
of ensuring that they would all remain in Oklahoma. So some
of the Cherokee simply walked back, and it is said that as
they walked, they collected those sacred tears, the corn
beads, from the ground on which they lay and used them to
make the Cherokee corn-bead necklace in remembrance and
honor of the Sacred Circle. Many of the people never again
returned to their beloved home. But the beauty remained in

their hearts, never to be lost, and never to be forgotten. And so, it is good.

Francene Hart ©92

CHAPTER FIVE

The Fire Still Burns

People must be born and reborn to belong.

—STANDING BEAR, LAKOTA CHIEF

In Cherokee tradition, there is a belief that at one time there were certain beings who came down from Galun'lati (Sky World) and formed Mother Earth, the sun, the moon, and the stars. These beings were said to have always existed in Galun'lati and to live there eternally. There were three beings: Uhalotega or Ogedoda (meaning "head of all power" or "great beyond expression"); Atunutitsu (meaning "place of uniting"); and Usgohula (referring to the lower part of the body). These three beings were sometimes referred to as Chota-auhnele-eh, meaning "Elder Fires Above" or "Red Thunder Beings." They were the Great One (Creator) and the Great One's two children, or helpers.

It is believed that the Great One created Sun and Moon, shaped Mother Earth, giving life to all living beings, and then returned to Galun'lati, leaving Sun and Moon to guard Earth. Fire was thought to have been given the responsibility of taking care of humankind, so when Cherokee people prayed, they always made an offering (usually tobacco) to the fire. The smoke that billowed upward from the fire was considered to be a messenger carrying the people's prayers to Sun and to the Creator.

The Sacred Fire, part of the first fire given to the people, was always kept burning as a sign of connection between Mother Earth and the sky, reaching upward to the Creator, and as a symbol of the Sacred Fire within—the heart (our connection with every living being). This fire was traditionally kept in the Council House and tended by a firekeeper, whose sole responsibility it was to protect and maintain the fire. This Sacred Fire was kept burning with seven specific kinds of wood, representing the seven clans of the Cherokee and the Seven Sacred Directions of the universe. The Council House, whose door opened to the east, was a seven-sided building that contained seven sections for the seven clans.

The seven clans of the Cherokee represented the Seven Sacred Directions of the universe required for harmonious existence. Each clan possessed a portion of the Medicine and offered a special contribution to the entire community/nation that was unique to that particular clan. Therefore, each clan relied on the other clans for survival in harmony and balance. The seven clans were (and are today):

1. Ani-Sahoni (Blue or Panther Clan, sometimes Wild Cat or Blue Holly)—known for making medicine from a special plant to keep children well.
2. Ani-Gilohi (Long Hair Clan, sometimes Twister or

Wind)—known for their responsibility as peacekeepers.

3. Ani-Tsi's-qua (Bird Clan)—known as messengers, keepers of the birds.

4. Ani-Wodi (Paint Clan)—makers of red paint, known as medicine people, and sometimes conjurers.

5. Ani-Awi (Deer Clan)—keepers of the deer, known as fast runners and hunters.

6. Ani-Gatogewi (Wild Potato Clan, sometimes Bear or Raccoon)—known for digging the wild potatoes to make flour for bread.

7. Ani-Waya (Wolf Clan)—keepers of the wolf, known as warriors.

There are different combinations of wood that were used for the Sacred Fire depending on what the fire was being used for and which woods were readily available in a particular area. The seven woods used in the Sacred Fire, as told to me by my father, included sycamore (East), beech (South), oak (West), birch or maple (North), pine (Center), locust (Above), and hickory (Below). Again, these types of woods might vary, but it was the intention and outcome that mattered most: things were to be done in a "proper way," respecting and offering reverence to the natural laws of Creation. This meant offering prayers to the Great One and to each of the Seven Sacred Directions.

From the center of the Circle represented by the Sacred Fire and our connection with the Great One, prayers were made to each of the Four Directions:

In the East: Iga-e-hinvdo, or Kalvgvi, or Nvda, or Egela, or Gigagi'i—the Red One, signifying the sun and sacred power

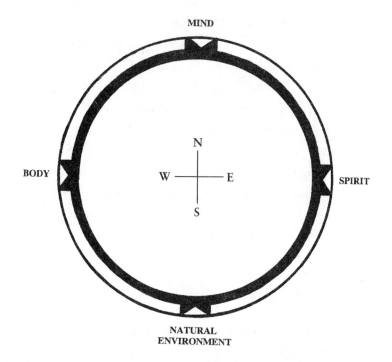

In the South: Tsuganawv'i, or Yehowa, or Dohiyi, or Unega—the White One (sometimes depicted with green or yellow), little spirit of peace and renewal

In the West: Wudeligv'i, or Ama, or Gvnagi'i—the fearless Black One of purity and strength

In the North: Tsuyvtlv'i, or Dohiyi, or Sagonige'i—the Blue One of truth and wisdom

The remaining directions were indicated in prayer referring to: Elohino, Mother Earth, offering the ground on which we walk; Galun'lati, the skyvault; and Ayehli or Adanvdo, the center that connects with all things, the Sacred Fire that burns within.

To this day, the Sacred Fire of the Cherokee burns continuously in Cherokee, North Carolina, and in Tahlequah, Oklahoma, not only as a connection with the past and all those who have walked before us, but as a present connection with the Great One and all living beings in the Greater Circle. And to this day, when the sound of thunder descends from Galŭn'lati, it is thought by many to be the joyous sound of the Thunder Beings beating their skydrum, celebrating life.

....

DONELAWEGA: THE POWWOW

Walk into the surrounding area of a powwow and you will be greeted by the fullness of color and sound and movement. You can feel the vibration of the drum, the rhythmic flow of the traditional singing in harmony with the falling of footsteps (and jingling of bells) as the dancers move in unison. You can see the numerous crafts and jewelry, among other things, being sold at the booths that surround the Circle, and you may catch occasional wafts of Indian frybread and powdered sugar. This is only part of what it is like to enter the Circle of a traditional "Donelawega," which in Cherokee simply means "a coming-together of people for a special purpose."

Purpose of the Powwow

Although the powwow originated with the Plains tribes, Native people across the United States have embraced the powwow as a traditional celebration of life and all our relations on Mother Earth. This has easily become a "pan-Indian" tradition as many tribes historically have ceremonial dances or similar traditions that bring people together for a specific purpose to be carried out communally. Traditionally, the powwow is an opportunity for a coming-together of people from different communities, tribes, or nations for the purpose of renewing old friendships, creating new friendships, celebrating our Native heritage, and feeling thankfulness at being alive with the beating of our hearts. Although the dancing and singing may appear as entertainment or a form of theatrics, the powwow experience has deep spiritual significance for many Native Americans, who believe that both the dancing and singing are a form of prayer and a sacred source of healing power, or Medicine.

The Drum: Heartbeat of Mother Earth

One of the most powerful forms of the Medicine, or life energy, resides with the drum, referred to as "grandmother" (or "grandfather"), whose resonance serves as a prayer to the Creator and to our ancestors, giving thanks for all of the gifts with which we are blessed every day. The drum consists not only of the instrument itself, but also includes the head singer and all other singers. Considered an elder, the drum is looked upon with great respect and dignity, representing the sacred heartbeat in all of us and the heartbeat of Mother Earth. Any person who approaches the drum must come with a sense of humility, refraining from the use of alcohol, drugs, or profanity, and that person must feel in his or her heart that he or she is no better than anyone else in the Circle.

Sacred Circle: Dance Arena

Dance arenas can be any open ground large enough to comfortably accommodate all participants and observers.

Before any of the activities have begun, the Circle is "blessed" in a traditional way by a spiritual leader, or medicine person. The powwow is then held within the realm of this sacred Circle, which represents the unity of all living beings in the Greater Circle of Life. Thus, the powwow serves not only as a social gathering in which people share good food, swap stories, and catch up on the latest news, but also serves as a symbolic gathering of all living beings in the harmony and balance of relationship on Mother Earth. So when we enter the Circle and the camaraderie of all our brothers and sisters, we come with a sense of humility, respect, excitement, and peace.

The Giveaway

It is common practice during a powwow for a "Giveaway" to be held. As a form of ceremony in itself, the Giveaway serves as a culturally appropriate means of displaying feelings of thankfulness by publicly "gifting" one's brothers and sisters. This might be done in a formal ceremony as a way of publicly honoring others, or it might be done in an informal, private manner.

Traditionally, it is a great honor to be able to gift someone. The recipients might be a certain small number of close persons, or they might be a large number of people who are in attendance. In the traditional way, one who gives in an unselfish manner, and without expectation, is a highly respected person. This is one who demonstrates reverence for all his or her relations by understanding his or her own place in the Greater Circle as a helper, who is there to experience life and to learn through generosity, respect, and humility.

....

WHY POSSUM'S TAIL IS BARE

A long time ago, when people could still understand the language of the animals, Ujetsdi, Possum, used to have a long, beautiful, bushy tail. In fact, he had the longest, most beautiful, bushiest tail of all of the animals—and he knew it. He was so proud of his tail that he liked to brush it every day, and he sang about it all the time.

The animals, who hadn't had a good powwow in awhile, decided that it was high time for a traditional "Donelawega," and they decided together in council that as part of the festivities, there would be a contest to see who had the most beautiful tail. Well, all of the animals knew who was going to win, but it was a good time to celebrate, eat well, offer prayers, see old friends, and make some new ones.

The council sent Tsi-s-du, Rabbit, as a messenger to bring news of the powwow to all of the animals in the different communities. Rabbit, who had had no tail since Bear had pulled it out, was very jealous of Possum and decided he was going to get Possum good.

So Rabbit eventually went to Possum's house and greeted him, telling about the powwow that was to be held and about the contest. "Can I tell the council that you will be at the powwow then?" asked Rabbit inquisitively.

"Oh, I'd love to come," responded Possum, "but you'll have to make sure that I have a special seat up front so that all of the animals can see my long, beautiful tail."

"I am sure that the council wouldn't *think* of having you sit anywhere else, Possum," chimed Rabbit. "After all, it would be such an honor to have you sitting up front where everyone could see your tail. I'll even have someone come to

brush and prepare it in a *proper* way since this is such a special event. After all, a tail that beautiful deserves a little special attention, and you want it to be done right."

Possum couldn't agree more and was very pleased, saying, "Oh, that would be just lovely. My tail is quite beautiful as it is, but I'm sure a little extra attention wouldn't hurt any."

So Rabbit went along his way and soon came upon Tolatsga, Cricket, who was considered an expert hair cutter by all the animals. Cricket happened to owe Rabbit a favor and it was time to pay up, so Rabbit told him just what to do and, once again, went about his business.

The next morning, Cricket went to Possum's house, saying that he had been sent by Rabbit to prepare Possum's tail for the powwow. So Possum, who had already been busy brushing his tail, stretched out on a big soft bed of moss and closed his eyes, while Cricket went to work. Cricket brushed Possum's tail (while Possum reminded him how beautiful it was) and told him he would wrap a long strip of red cloth around and around it to keep it smooth until the powwow. But all the while, without Possum knowing it, Cricket was clipping the hair off Possum's tail all the way down to the roots!

That night Possum went to the ceremonial grounds where the powwow was being held. All of the animals were there. Each of the clans came in one by one. First to arrive was Uwohali, Eagle, and all those in the Bird Clan from the east, bringing a piece of the Sacred Fire. You could hear their wings flapping silently as they all came in with a *whoosh*.

Then the little plants and trees came in from the south, bringing wood and tobacco for the Fire. Gvli, Raccoon, came too, but he was late because he got held up in a tree by a honeycomb. Doyi, Beaver, wasn't far behind, sporting all kinds of welts from bee stings he had somehow gotten during the course of the day.

Then from the west came the Bear Clan, with the solid thudding sound of bear paws hitting the ground and the soft rumble of bear growls. Yonv, the bears, brought the powwow drum and a big sack of water to control the Fire.

And, finally, from the north came Awi, the Deer Clan, entering the circle with quiet observation, grace, and gentleness. Tawodi, Hawk, came with them, too, bringing a little wind for the fire. And so, all of the animals came in a little at a time and gathered together. Before long, bears were on the powwow drum, and you could feel the vibration all the way to the heart, while the birds sang songs in unison and Gogv, Crow, made his special calls to accent the songs.

Then one at a time the animals danced into the Circle, around the Sacred Fire, and showed their tails to the admiring community. And there was Possum, sitting right up front in his special seat just as Rabbit had promised, waiting for his turn, which would be last. Patiently he waited, noticing how other animals' tails were no match for the beauty of his own. One by one, the animals moved into the Circle and then out once again: first Eagle, then Raccoon, then Bear, then Deer, and so on, until all of the animals had had their turn. And then it came time for Possum.

Possum loosened the red cloth tied around his tail and danced elegantly into the Circle, singing, "Behold my beautiful tail! See how long and beautiful it is! See the way it shines!" Then he wiggled his tail for all the animals to see.

The animals roared, and Possum continued dancing around the Circle, again singing, "Behold my beautiful tail! See how long and beautiful it is! See the way it sweeps the air!" And again he wiggled his tail for all the animals to see.

Once more, the animals roared in laughter, and in response, Possum's voice resonated even louder than before, "Behold my beautiful tail! See how long and beautiful it is! See how fine the fur is!" And once again he wiggled his tail for all the animals to see.

By now the animals were laughing so hard that Possum began to wonder why. As he looked around, everyone was laughing and pointing at his tail. Possum peered behind him and saw to his surprise that there was no hair on his tail—it was completely bald! Well, he was so shocked and embarrassed that without saying a word, he fell to the ground and played dead. And to this day, when taken by surprise, Possum does this. And to this day, Possum's tail is still bare. And so, it is good.

CHAPTER SIX

Walking in Step with The Greater Circle

*You have noticed that everything an Indian does is
in a circle, and that is because the Power of the
World always works in circles, and everything tries
to be round. . . . The sky is round, and I have heard
that Earth is round like a ball, and so are all the
stars. The wind, in its greatest power, whirls. Birds
make their nests in circles, for theirs is the same religion as ours. . . . Even the seasons form a great circle in their changing, and always come back again to
where they were. The life of a person is a circle from
childhood to childhood, and so it is in everything
where power moves.*

—BLACK ELK, OGLALA LAKOTA MEDICINE MAN

Many Native peoples have historically believed not only that Earth is round, but also that, by the very nature of the universe, Mother Earth moves in cycles. These cycles reflect the continuous "Circle of Life." All life moves within this Circle, and all life exists by virtue of the many circles, or cycles. All of life is in constant motion like the flowing waters of a stream; all of life is interrelated and interdependent as the many intricate threads of a single web.

An understanding and appreciation of our natural surroundings is central to Native American cultures. Mother Earth moves and breathes and flows, comprised of many intricately balanced and interdependent cycles that allow for the continuity of life. Each day Sun rises in the east, slowly working his way across the sky until, by the end of the day, he reaches the west and drops below the horizon, only to appear once again the following day. Rain falls from the sky, then evaporates into the clouds above Mother Earth, only to fall again in a continuation of the cycle. Similarly, the four seasons form a great circular motion as they change and repeat their cycles, bringing birth and rebirth.

Because humans are a part of nature and nature is known to move in cycles, many Native Americans believe that we, too, move in cycles. As a sacred symbol, the Circle is a reminder that what we often see as progression or growth is, indeed, circular in nature or, rather, cyclical, representing a spiraling motion that can take on a particular direction through choice.

Circles of life energy surround us, exist within us, and make up the many relationships of our existence. We each have a circle of self, comprised of the many facets of our own development (e.g., mind, body, spirit); a circle of immediate family, extended family, tribal family, community, and nation; and a circle consisting of the natural environment and our universal surroundings.

Related to the Circle of Life is the belief that all things are alive, all things have spiritual energy, and, hence, all things are of essential importance within the Circle. From this belief stems the reverence of Native American peoples for life in all its forms: animals, plants, rocks and minerals, people, Mother Earth, sky, sun, moon, stars, wind, water, fire, thunder, lightning, and rain. All life exists in an intricate system of interdependence, so that the universe exists in a dynamic state of harmony and balance, reflecting the continuous flow and cycling of energy that emanates from each form of life in relation to every other living being. The interdependence of all energy cycles reflects a belief, related by Chief Seattle, that "all things are connected like the blood which unites one family;" hence, all life is worthy of respect and reverence.

The components of the Circle of Life, depicted as the ordinal compass points in the Circle, include mind, body, spirit, and the natural environment as a way of representing the aspects of Medicine. As mentioned in chapter 4, in Native American culture the term "Medicine" refers to "the essence of life or an inner power" that creates every living being's particular way of life and presence. This is a way that is chosen in spirit and lived out in physical form so that a person may learn in mind, body, *and* spirit. Our choice of the way in which we focus our time and energies in each of the directions reflects our values and priorities.

Understanding life energy, how to respect and maintain

that energy, and how to use that energy are all parts of the Medicine. Being in harmony and balance means moving in step with the universe and with its sacred rhythms—this is what many Indian people refer to as Good Medicine. By contrast, being in disharmony or "dis-ease" means being out of step with the universe and its sacred rhythms, therefore inviting illness. Disharmony results when we are out of balance, our energies are unfocused or poorly focused, and we lose sight of our place in the Greater Circle.

Well-being occurs when we seek and find our unique place in the universe and experience the continuous cycle of receiving and giving through respect and reverence for the beauty of all living things. Stated another way, everyone and everything was created with a specific purpose to fulfill, and no one should have the power to interfere or impose on others the best path to follow. Our chosen way of life shows how we focus our energies and how we seek a sense of harmony and balance among the interaction and interrelation of the Four Directions in relation to other living beings.

Thus, the wellness of the mind, body, spirit, and natural environment is an expression of the proper balance in the relationship of all things. If one disturbs or disrupts the natural balance of relationship, illness in any of the four areas may be the result. This is one of the primary reasons for keeping one's life energy strong and clear in relation to others and the natural environment.

In many Native American languages, there is no word for "religion" because spiritual practices are an integral part of every aspect of daily life; they are necessary for the harmony and balance, or wellness, of the individual, family, clan, and community. Healing and worship are considered one and the same. For many Native American people, the concept of health and wellness is not only a physical state, but a spiritual one as well. Carol Locust, Eastern Band of Cherokee, has described a number of traditional beliefs concerning wellness and unwellness (*Harvard Educational Review* 58, no. 3, pp. 317–318):

1. Traditional Native Americans believe in a Creator, sometimes referred to as Great Creator, Great Spirit, or Great One, among other names.
2. Human beings are made up of spirit, mind, and body.
3. Plants and animals, like humans, are part of the spirit world. The spirit world exists side by side with, and intermingles with, the physical world.
4. The spirit existed before it came into a physical body and will exist after the body dies.
5. Illness affects the mind and spirit as well as the body.
6. Wellness is harmony in spirit, mind, and body.
7. Unwellness is disharmony in spirit, mind, and body.
8. Natural unwellness is caused by the violation of a sacred social or natural law of Creation.
9. Unnatural unwellness is caused by conjuring (witchcraft) from those with destructive intentions.
10. Each of us is responsible for his or her own wellness.

Traditional Native American views of health and wellness emphasize the necessity of seeking harmony within oneself, with others, and with one's surroundings. They emphasize an active relationship between the physical and the spirit worlds and the necessity of seeking harmony and balance in both. For many Native American people, wellness through spirituality is not a *part* of life, it *is* life. In our terminology, this means "walking the path of Good Medicine" (living a good way of life) "in harmony and balance" (through the harmonious interaction of mind, body, spirit, and natural environment) "with all our relations" (with all living beings in the Circle of Life).

....

THE TALKING CIRCLE: A TRADITIONAL COMING-TOGETHER

Native Americans have long used the Circle to celebrate the sacred interrelationship we all share with one another and with our world. Old Western movies conjure up images of the "Indians" sitting together in council in the Circle, while they make decisions about whether or not to go to war with the "White man." But the Circle is more far reaching than could be portrayed in the movies.

The idea of the council or the "Talking Circle" permeates the traditions of Native Americans to this day. It symbolizes an entire approach to life and to the universe in which each being participates in the Circle and each one serves an important and necessary function that is valued no more or no less than that of any other being. By honoring the Circle, we as human beings honor the process of life and the process of growth that is an ever-flowing stream in the movement of life energy.

Many Native Americans consider the whole greater than the sum of its parts. Traditionalists have always believed that healing and transformation should take place in the presence of the group since we are all related to one another in very basic ways; we can always use the support and insight of our fellow brothers and sisters as we move away from something and toward something else. In this way, the ceremonial Circle has served a very sacred function through the ritual healing or cleansing of body, mind, and spirit, while also serving as a way of bringing people together. Each person comes to the Circle as a human being with his or her own concerns, and together participants seek harmony and balance by sharing stories, praying, singing, talking, and sometimes even just sitting together in silence.

The Circle is a sacred reminder of the interrelationship, respect, and clarity that come from opening oneself up to the energy of the Circle of Life—the wisdom offered by one's experiences, the experiences of others, and the world in which we live. The Circle is a sacred symbol reminding us of the importance of our unique place in the universe and our relation with all things. In a traditional Native American "coming-together," the Talking Circle fulfills an important purpose by ensuring that relations are conducted in a very respectful manner. It traditionally serves as a forum for the expression of thoughts and feelings in a context of complete acceptance by participants.

To begin, in Cherokee tradition, participants form a circle together, leaving an opening in the direction of the east, which is where the sun rises, bringing with it clarity and honesty. A traditional chant with music, rattle, or drumming may be used for relaxation and clearing of mind, body, and spirit as people enter the circle. When everyone has gathered, initial greetings are made. As is done in the traditional way, this is time for "visiting" or maybe sharing some food together. When it is time for the Talking Circle to begin, the "talking stick" (or other ceremonial object) is passed following a ceremonial "Clearing Way" to literally clear the way for Good Medicine to come into the Circle.

The talking stick is generally used in the group as a sacred object representing truth and understanding as powerful agents of healing (other objects such as the eagle feather may also be used). The talking stick is a wooden stick—usually made from mountain laurel in Cherokee tradition—embellished with symbolic carvings or paintings, and prepared in a special way to ward off disharmony. The "medicine object," as it is sometimes called, signifies permission to speak (by way of whoever holds it). Thus, use of the medicine object gives each person a chance to speak and encourages each member to listen more carefully without need for competition. Traditionally in many Native American tribes, people used the talking stick during council meetings to discuss issues or concerns peacefully by "speaking from the heart" and by listening intently to what others had to say.

The facilitator, who traditionally might be a social or spiritual leader or respected elder, begins by picking up the talking stick to share feelings or concerns with the group. Humor is almost always an important part of this entire process as a way of bringing people together. When the facilitator has spoken, the talking stick is passed clockwise (left) to the next person, who may choose to speak or to remain silent. Then the talking stick is passed to each person.

It is made clear that the stick holder may not be interrupted or criticized. During the circle, questions may be asked, with verbal exchanges taking place, but only with the permission of whoever is holding the stick. Another member wishing to speak about something not related to what the "stick holder" is talking about must wait his or her turn. The facilitator is free to ask questions or make clarifying statements, but, again, only with permission. Statements directed to other members are encouraged to be framed as "I statements" using feelings or ideas. In this way, an atmosphere of patience and respect is cultivated, freeing members to experience transformation and healing in the group.

When the talking stick has made at least two or three go-arounds, having been passed to all participants, it is laid in the center of the circle to be picked up by anyone wishing to speak further. When all those who want to speak are finished, the Talking Circle is brought to a close with a traditional chant, prayer, or Blessing Way (ceremonial expression of gratitude and humility) to give thanks for the coming-together. It is understood that what has been said in the circle remains in the circle to demonstrate respect for all members and to protect the sacredness of the experience.

Whether the Circle is a ceremonial circle, a powwow, a spiritual gathering, or even the sharing of a meal, the traditional sense of belonging and comfort does provide healing and Medicine for all; the Circle reminds us of life and our place in it. As one Cherokee elder put it, "This is our time to be together. Food is always welcomed, but our connection with each other and with the Great One is what counts. The Circle never ends, even though people come and go, so our coming-together is for a greater meaning and purpose than just a meeting or a time to share food and conversation." The Circle always reminds us of our ability to make ourselves available to the energy and peace of life, even when this seems impossible.

Francene Hart

CHAPTER SEVEN

The Rule of Opposites

*The good road and the road of difficulties, you
have made me cross; and where they cross, the
place is holy.*

—BLACK ELK, OGLALA LAKOTA MEDICINE MAN

Traditionally, stories like that of Sun and Moon (in chapter 1) remind us of the sacred relationship between opposite energies. This is the way to understanding and respecting the beauty and simplicity that exist in the Circle. Basic teachings such as these guided the lives of those who lived in the traditional way. Across tribal nations there were specific people or groups within the tribe who played an important role in this process. It was their responsibility to remind others of the power of harmony and balance through their way of life.

....

CRAZY DOGS AND THE CONTRARY WAY

Historically, sacred societies were organized and strictly regulated with both a social and a spiritual function to be carried out for their tribal communities. In addition, smaller societies were sometimes created by those who, for whatever reason, did not qualify for the larger, more established societies.

For instance, among the Pawnee and some other tribes, the "Contrary Society," or what was sometimes referred to as the "Crazy Dogs," was one of the smaller societies formed following a vision by the leaders. Organized around certain ceremonies and specified ways of doing things, the members painted themselves black, indicating that they were always ready to fight, and reversed normal expectations for behavior. In *This Land Was Theirs*, anthropologist Wendall Oswalt describes the process:

> If the camp were attacked, they continued whatever they were doing before the alarm; if someone told them not to go on a raid, they went; and if a mysterious animal which normal persons feared were near the camp, they hunted it. (p. 237)

Thus, the Crazy Dogs emphasized a very important lesson for all of the members of their tribal community to witness. Indeed, says Cherokee elder Dhyani Ywahoo in *Voices of Our Ancestors*,

> the one who disagrees with you is serving a sacred purpose in showing you the limitation of form. Such a person may be a "contrary" or "thunder being" who inspires deeper understanding. (p. 124)

The Crazy Dogs dedicated themselves to a life of the opposite, and they were highly revered as holy persons who always reminded people of the opposite that is implied in any action, thought, or feelings. And they did their people a great justice. By doing the opposite of every behavior that was considered to be right or true, the Crazy Dogs emphasized the importance of perspective, thus creating a balance in the greater social and spiritual order. Moreover, they achieved considerable prestige for their bravery and for remaining true to their cause by following their vision, though among the Pawnee, their numbers dwindled to the point of disbanding after a battle in which most of the members were killed. (The other warriors had probably called a retreat.)

EXERCISE: Crazy Dog

Just for fun, select a time, a place, and who you want your "victims" to be, then do just the opposite of what everyone expects of you or what you have always expected of yourself. Take care not to harm anyone or yourself in completing this exercise, but do toss all cares to the wind and live a little on the Crazy Dog side, as does Turtle in the following story.

....

WHY TURTLE'S SHELL IS SCARRED

One day, Ujetsdi, Possum, and Daksi, Turtle, decided to go find some delicious plums. They walked together for quite a way until they came upon a tree full of ripe plums. Possum, who was a good climber now that his tail had no hair to get in the way, climbed quickly up the tree and began throwing the plums down to Turtle.

Before long, Waya, Wolf, came along, and since he was very hungry, he got right in the way of Turtle and started gulping down the plums one at a time as they were being tossed from the tree. Turtle was too slow for Wolf, who was getting a kick out of the fact that he was getting the best of Possum and Turtle. So Possum waited for the perfect opportunity and threw a large plum down that got lodged in Wolf's throat and choked him to death.

Turtle gathered up the remaining plums scattered all about the ground, saying, "You know, Possum, I hate for such a fine wolf to go to waste. I think I'll take his ears so that I can use them for hominy spoons." So Turtle went over to Wolf and cut off his ears. Then he went on his way, while Possum stayed up in the tree with sticky plum juice running down his chin.

Soon, Turtle came to the house of Tiyoha'li, Lizard, who invited him in for some corn broth. Turtle accepted graciously, and the two of them ate together. Sitting in the warmth of the afternoon sunshine, Turtle dipped spoonful after spoonful using Wolf's ear as a spoon. Lizard noticed this and wondered about it, but he said nothing. When Turtle had had his fill of corn broth, he thanked Lizard and went on his way. When he came to Porcupine's house later on and again was invited to share some corn broth, he once again pulled out Wolf's ear and used it as a spoon to dip his broth with.

Well, before long word had gotten around that Turtle had killed Wolf and was using his ears as spoons. When the wolves heard about this, they were outraged, and all went after Turtle to settle things once and for all. When the wolves finally caught up with him, they made Turtle prisoner while

they held council in order to decide what to do to him. At first, the wolves decided to boil Turtle in a clay pot, so they brought the pot and prepared it. But as they were getting everything ready, Turtle only laughed at it, saying, "If you put me in that clay pot, I'll just kick it to pieces—but you can do that to me if you really want to."

This frustrated the wolves who held council again, and

this time they decided that they would burn Turtle in the fire. So they prepared the wood, but as they were about to light it up, Turtle only laughed, saying, "If you put me in the fire, I'll just put it out—but you can do that to me if you really want to."

Now the wolves, who were running out of ideas, held council again, and they decided that they would throw him in the deepest hole in the river and drown him. Turtle trembled in horror and pleaded with the wolves, begging them, "Oh no, please not that—anything but that!" But the wolves paid no attention to him. They dragged him to the riverbank and threw him in. That, of course, was just what Turtle had been waiting for all along. As he fell with a huge splash into the water, he swam under the water to the other side of the river and got away.

But it has been said that when the wolves threw him into the river, Turtle fell on a big river rock under the water that cracked his shell in twelve places. Some say that he sang a medicine song:

> I have sewn myself together,
> I have sewn myself together,
> I have sewn myself together,
> I have sewn myself together.

And the power of the song was so great that the pieces came together, but the scars remained on his back, and you can still see them to this day. And so, it is good.

....

THE RULE OF OPPOSITES

Because of the traditional Native American emphasis on the concept of the Circle, what would otherwise be perceived as opposites or dualities on a linear continuum are thought of as actually existing in a circle that has no real beginning or end. Thus, in the traditional way, terms such as *good* and *bad* are seldom used in their pure or extreme sense, but rather they are given a relative value since it is believed that one naturally implies the other. Truth lies somewhere *between* the two poles, rather than at *one* of the two poles. This concept is called the "Rule of Opposites." Using the Circle, it is believed to be more important for a person to look beyond surface value, such as good or bad, in order to seek what is true. In the traditional way, understanding of the Rule of Opposites facilitates the recognition of meaning and truth, which provides a means of walking in step with the Circle, seeking purpose and direction in life.

There are grave differences between an approach emphasizing "this and that" and the approach emphasizing "this or that" or, in the extreme, "this *versus* that." It is the oppositional nature of the latter two approaches that can result in discordant feelings, thoughts, and actions. Many times in life we speak about the importance of intention or attitude, and how this can make all the difference in the world—the idea that "attitude is everything." In the traditional way, intention is critical. It is considered to be as significant as, if not more important than, the act itself because in Cherokee teachings, intention *is* the act itself—the thought as well as the act constitutes Nuwati, the Medicine. That is why harmony and balance are so important in the traditional way. There is no such thing as keeping the mountains and getting rid of the valleys; they are one and the same, and they exist because of one another.

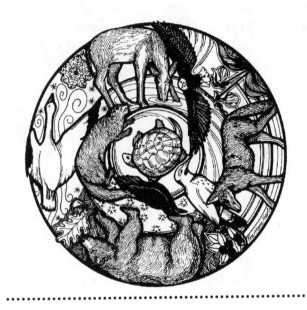

···

SEVEN LIFE LESSONS

The Rule of Opposites helps us understand our Medicine by helping us to understand our actions and our intentions. This rule emphasizes the central role of choice in the traditional view of life, and it includes seven key life lessons:

1. Opposites are extensions of themselves, like two opposing hands of the same body; one opposite implies the other.
2. We choose our own (discordant) opposites wherein *we* are the true source of the difficulty we experience.
3. Everything serves a meaningful and important function in our lives.
4. Asking the right questions, instead of asking for the right answers, allows us to know the *function* rather than the *effect* of our choices.

5. Questioning our assumptions allows us to recognize underlying meanings or truths and the relative value of choices made.
6. Understanding underlying truths eliminates any need for discord in our lives.
7. Through choice of perspective and appropriate action, we are free to balance ourselves as we see fit.

Lesson 1

Opposites are extensions of themselves, like two opposing hands of the same body; one opposite implies the other.

The nature of opposites is, simply stated, that both opposites are true. For every *is*, there is an *isn't*. The only true difference between these positions lies in the unique perspective of the individual. One person looks at the Circle and sees *is*, while another person looks at the same Circle and sees *isn't*. However, both are true; both persons are "correct" in their perceptions. *Is* and *isn't* are not really opposite poles on a linear continuum, but rather they exist in a circle, where one is an extension of the other. *Is* exists as an extension of *isn't*; one begins where the other leaves off. One opposite implies the other, as the following excerpt from Margaret Craven's *I Heard the Owl Call My Name* illustrates:

> All day long he moved down the longest, the loveliest of all the inlets, and it seemed to him that something strange happened to time. When he had first come to the village, it was the future that loomed huge. So much to plan. So much to learn. Then it was the present that had consumed him—

each day with all its chores and never enough hours to do them. Now time had lost its contours. He seemed to see it as the raven or the bald eagle, flying high over the village, must see the part of the river that had passed the village, that had not yet reached the village, one and the same. (p. 148)

From the perspective of the raven or eagle, the vision of the river in motion, in spite of location, remains the same. Where the river is moving to and where the river is moving from are less important than the motion itself. Different parts of the river do not exist on a linear continuum, but rather in a circle, wherein one part of the river is merely an extension of another; all is connected in flow.

Similarly, the question "Who am I?" automatically implies the opposite question, "Who am I not?" Likewise, "What did I do?" implies the question "What did I not do?" Opposites are thus an inherent part of any given experience. They may be seen as extensions of one another, like two opposing hands of the same body.

Lesson 2

We choose our own (discordant) opposites wherein we are the true source of the difficulty we experience.

Because many people are not consciously aware of the existence of opposites, they may make choices that create disharmony. Conflict, whether intrapsychic or interpersonal, seems to be an ever-present part of the human condition, such that a search for resolution of conflicts is an ever-present and natural part of living. According to the traditional Native American way, however, the idea of conflict is in itself an illusion. Essentially, as Dhyani Ywahoo puts it in *Voices of Our Ancestors* (p. 44), "All is vibration [or energy], and what has the appearance of conflict is better understood as dissonance or discord, energies seeking resolution in harmony".

All things are made up of energy. Thoughts and feelings, for example, are nothing more than energy. Through the choices we make, our thoughts and feelings, and even our actions, take on a distinctive nature according to the direction in which they are moved.

Vectors (represented by arrows) are used in physics to depict both the direction and magnitude of energy. Vectors also can be applied to thoughts and feelings. For example, feelings of joy or sadness are nothing more than energy of a particular magnitude. It is not until a choice is made, be it ever so slight as a choice in perspective, that the energies making up the feelings of joy or sadness take on direction, thus becoming joy or sadness, and the tears that flow from either. In actuality, these opposite feelings are one and the same—nothing more than energy that has been assigned a direction through choice.

Similarly, conflict is nothing more than energy that has been assigned a direction through choice. We choose the discordant opposites that become the source of our "problems" or, rather, "energies seeking resolution in harmony." Unfortunately, because we may not be aware that we often have more choices available to us than we realize, we make choices that may not prove to be useful or constructive in the short or long term. As perspectives change, however, hindsight may reveal that a greater array of choices was indeed possible. The challenge, then, is to achieve a greater range of perspective in the moment. This is what some refer to as wisdom. It is never the energies themselves that are the source of our problems but, rather, our understanding and use of these energies.

Lesson 3

Everything serves a meaningful and important function in our lives.

Many of the old stories and legends relate a number of basic life lessons. One lesson frequently conveyed through story is the idea that everything and everyone has a specific purpose on Mother Earth. As my grandmother put it, "Don't ever try to be what you're not, but don't ever let anyone else tell you what you are either." In a real sense, everything and everyone possesses intrinsic value or worth by merely existing in the Circle of Life. This intrinsic worth extends to experience as well. In other words, every experience also possesses intrinsic worth by the very fact that it occurred, and therefore it is a gift of sorts.

You will hear many "waiting" stories from people who are waiting for life to happen. They are waiting to grow up, waiting to find the perfect mate, waiting for the right job, waiting for their kids to grow up, waiting for retirement, and so on. However, life is meant to be lived, and every experience is to be experienced fully as a gift. Everything happens with a purpose. Every experience thus offers a unique opportunity to learn and grow in ways that would not be possible without all of our experiences, both good and bad. Therefore, there is no real right or wrong way to do things, in that one may learn something valuable no matter how things are done.

Lesson 4

Asking the right questions, instead of asking for the right answers, allows us to know the function *rather than the* effect *of our choices.*

The following is a commonly posed question that reflects one's outlook on life: "Is the glass half-empty or half-full?" This question presupposes that the answer can be only one of two possibilities. However, the Rule of Opposites, as I heard one elder put it, poses a different question altogether: "Is the glass the right size?" After all, it might be too big or too small. This is just one example of the way in which we limit ourselves through our perception of choice.

The Rule of Opposites thus provides a reminder to clarify one's assumptions by asking the right questions rather than seeking the right answers. For example, when faced with a decision between the unacceptable and the undesirable, many people often focus on the choice between what seems to be the "lesser of two evils." However, a change in perspective may focus on a different question, such as, "Does this situation represent a deeper lesson (truth) for me than what I perceive right now?" Rather than understanding the situation as a limitation, one could be helped to see an opportunity.

Looking at decisions as a set of opposites on a linear continuum may lead a person away from understanding the continuum itself—in other words, the true meaning of a given situation or experience. For example, one who is angry may invest considerable energy in defending why someone made him or her upset. An alternate course of action would be to examine the energy of his or her discord and to clarify the underlying meaning of his or her feelings.

Questions that could stimulate an examination of the *function* rather than the *effect* of the choice to be angry could be, "In what way is my anger useful for me?" "What function does my anger serve for me?" "What does my anger mean to me?" The answers to these questions may reveal the true source of one's anger and the basis for the choice of this reaction in these particular circumstances, as well as overall patterns therein. At the same time, the question of what other choices one might make naturally arises, as possibilities present themselves.

Lesson 5

Questioning our assumptions allows us to recognize underlying meanings or truths and the relative value of choices made.

In the Medicine Way, everyone and everything is believed to possess universal purpose, since each has a place in the Circle. Hence, it is important to seek the underlying meanings of experiences rather than make surface judgments about them that may cloud our perceptions. The Rule of Opposites encourages us to clarify the assumptions on which we are acting, rather than focusing so much energy on *justifying* our actions and perceptions.

We, as human beings, possess the ability to reflect on our feelings, thoughts, and actions. Although we are able to view circumstances from multiple frames of reference, we sometimes fail to do so. When we ask a question, we need to include in our focus both the opposite of that question and an alternate question or questions that turn our focus to what is "true" rather than what is "right" or "wrong," "good" or "bad." For example, the question "What did you say?" implies the opposite question, "What did you not say?" These are both equally important questions, and part of the same truth.

A focus on either or even both questions, however, will not reveal the assumptions underlying what was said or not said. An alternate question is required to reveal the personal choice that was made and the personal value of that choice. "How did you come to make that choice?" and "What does it mean to you?" are questions that seek to clarify the underlying assumption more than the outcome (or even cause) of a decision or action.

Lesson 6

Understanding underlying truths eliminates any need for discord in our lives.

We are sometimes faced with a decision between the unacceptable and the undesirable. This is a natural part of living. It can also create a lot of internal conflict that need not occur. Every decision requires that we consider many complicated factors and carefully weigh our options. You have probably run into people whom I call, somewhat jokingly, the "yes buts." For every positive statement or resolution, they have a "yes, but . . ." The "yes buts" always have a reason not to do something or not to see something another way. They end up spending a lot of time and energy being stuck. It is important to remember, in defense of the "yes buts," that change can be very frightening for all of us.

Since all things are connected like the many strands of a web and everything in the Circle of Life affects everything else, we need to develop a greater understanding of our unique place and purpose in the universe. We need to step beyond our individual frame of reference to recognize deeper meanings and lessons that present themselves to us. Reacting to life circumstances without pausing for reflection limits our ability to perceive underlying truths through multiple perspectives. Sometimes it is important to have faith, sometimes it is important to have imagination.

In the traditional way, the idea of seeking resolution of dissonance and discord really encompasses a seeking of harmony and balance among interrelated thoughts, feelings, and actions. Recognizing the relationship or commonality among things is key to experiencing a sense of harmony and balance, which occurs when one recognizes and honors universal truths and underlying meanings.

Lesson 7

Through choice of perspective and appropriate action, we are free to balance ourselves as we see fit.

In the Medicine Way, living a life of harmony and balance does not mean living a life without challenges, difficulties, hardships, and even conflict. What it does mean is making constructive and creative choices through clear intention (wisdom) to fulfill one's purpose in the Greater Circle of Life by maintaining and contributing to the reciprocal balance of family, clan, tribe, and community in the context of personal, social, and natural environments.

Imagine the effect on a still lake when a pebble drops through the glassy surface. Cycles of energy radiate from the point of impact in ripples that extend and return in a cyclic motion until harmony (or balance) is renewed upon the lake's surface as the former state of stillness (imperceptible motion). Says Dhyani Ywahoo in *Voices of Our Ancestors* (p. 34), "Sleeping mind perceives the ripples as challenges of life; awakened mind sees them as ripples on a lake. Human beings have a particular opportunity to realize the arising nature of the mind, mind's creative nature, and to generate those thoughts and actions which are beneficial to harmony and balance".

Where one may perceive the everlasting difficulties that life presents as disruptive waves, another may perceive only ripples on a lake. The difference in perception reflects a difference in choice of action or reaction. There is an old anecdote that illustrates this point: Once while acting as a guide for a hunting expedition, a Native American could not find the way home. One of the men with him said, "You're lost, Chief." The Native American replied, "I'm not lost—my tepee is lost."

The Circle of Life moves by the energy of choice and learning. Each choice requires us to seek our place within the Circle, a place that balances the opposite pull of spiritual (spirit) and physical (body), mental (mind) and natural. Life consists of a continuing series of choices that present us with challenges to be met or ignored, consequences to be accepted or rejected. Because we have the freedom to choose, we also possess the freedom to seek a unique personal balance in our lives—or to maintain a state of disequilibrium. Inherent in either way, however, is the opportunity to learn and to understand. The primary lesson of the Rule of Opposites is the lesson of choice in moving toward calm and healing.

We attract those who teach us what we most need to learn, we teach ourselves through the choices we make and the consequences we must face, and we teach others through our experience in the way that we live. It takes a very strong spirit to endure the adversity of a difficult situation or experience. And when we are going through a difficult experience, we must continue to ask ourselves two things:

1. What is this experience teaching me about myself, about others, and about living?
2. What am I teaching others through my experience in the way that I live?

Spirit never dies unless it chooses to die, and even then it is a false death filled with important truths. Spirit never reaches calm until it decides that it is ready for this. Either way, spirit learns, spirit remembers, and spirit chooses.

....

THE MEDICINE OF THE EAGLE FEATHER

The eagle feather, which represents duality, tells the story of life through the seven lessons. It tells of the many dualities or opposites that exist in the Circle of Life, such as light and dark, male and female, substance and shadow, summer and winter, life and death, peace and war. The eagle feather has both light and dark colors, indicating seeming dualities and opposites (lesson 1). Though one can make a choice to argue about which of the colors is most beautiful or most valuable (lesson 2), the truth is that both colors come from the same feather, both are true, both are connected, and it takes both to fly (lesson 3).

The colors are opposite, but they are part of the same truth. The importance of the feather lies not in which color is most beautiful, but in finding out and accepting the purpose of the feather as a whole (lesson 4). Traditionally, one earns the eagle feather through enormous acts of courage, understanding, compassion, and generosity. Often, it is through acts such as these that we transcend our ordinarily limited state of being and begin to recognize the commonality (rather than oppositional separateness) of things as well as their intrinsic value and underlying truths (lesson 5). Through acts such as these, a recognition of universal oneness or truth occurs, and universal learning takes place. An honoring of underlying meanings, choice, and the interrelationship of all things in the Circle of Life emerges (lesson 6).

Native American tradition thus recognizes the oneness of differing phenomena through the metaphor of the eagle feather with its duality of colors. A decision or choice is made to honor both through harmony and balance, as it is only through harmony and balance that universal truths may be perceived and experienced (lesson 7). It is only through maintaining the harmony and balance of our feathers that we are able to fly.

My father, J.T. Garrett, Eastern Band of Cherokee, has spoken wisely about the lessons of the eagle feather in Steven McFadden's *Profiles in Wisdom*:

> The Eagle feather teaches us about the Rule of Opposites, about everything being divided into two ways. The more one is caught up in the physical, or the West, then

the more one has to go in the opposite direction, the East, or the spiritual, to get balance. And it works the other way too— you can't just focus on the spiritual to the exclusion of the physical. You need harmony in all Four Directions. (p. 173)

EXERCISE: Peace Treaty

This is a very simple exercise in harmony and yet perhaps as difficult as living life can be. Begin by making a list of what you would have to *do* in your life in order to come to your peace. Be specific, and be honest. Next, state beside each one what is preventing you from doing it as well as what it would take for you to overcome this barrier.

Focus on those things that you have control over or potentially could have control over given some things being changed. As you are making your list, be sure to distinguish between those things that are truly within your control and those things that are not truly within your control. Be careful about needing other people to change in order for you to come to your peace; this is putting the responsibility of your peace onto others, over whom you have no control. I don't waste my time trying to change people who don't want to change. Rather, I have learned that sometimes it is important to just get out of their way (Rule of Acceptance).

Also, be careful about the phrases "I wish . . ." or "If only . . . ," focusing rather on "I will . . . ," "I am going to . . . ," and "I want to . . ." Now do whatever it is that you have listed for yourself, being sure not to create harm for others or harm for yourself in completing these things. You have made your own peace treaty with yourself. Now, fulfill it.

CHAPTER EIGHT

Being and Doing

A raccoon's toughest job is simply to be.
—RACCOON, ANIMAL TRIBE, PHILOSOPHER AND CONNOISSEUR
OF FINE FOODS

It was a beautiful, warm summer day in the Great Smoky Mountains. Grandfather Sun poured his golden warmth graciously down upon the land for all of Mother Earth's creatures to enjoy. The air was crisp and alive with its own sacred dance, smoothly breathing life into everything. All the leaves were green and young, and the rivers and creeks flowed freely with cool, fresh mountain water.

Gvli, Raccoon, noticed all of this beauty as he sipped some of the cool, sparkling water from one of the nearby streams. *Ah, this really hits the spot!* Today was one of those days when Raccoon just couldn't seem to get to everything fast enough as he went from flower to flower, leaf to leaf, rock to rock, and back to the flowers again, exploring all of Mother Earth's vast wealth. Raccoon's little black-and-white nose always seemed to have a little bit of everything rubbed on it—by accident, of course. But Raccoon didn't really mind and hardly even noticed since there was so much to enjoy. Even the most cleverly concealed hiding place was unsafe from Raccoon's probing little snout. The discovery of some tasty morsel such as wild blackberries occasionally halted the journey, but only long enough for Raccoon to chew—and maybe to take a few for later.

Raccoon always made sure to put a little extra of whatever he found into his special pouch that he carried around his neck. After all, you never know when you might want to share a little something with someone else or have a small afternoon snack. And, as was the traditional way, Raccoon always gave thanks for whatever Elohino, Mother Earth, provided; he gave thanks to the plant people and the Great Creator. He always gave something in return as well, such as a little pinch of tobacco.

And so, Raccoon slowly made his way down the path to the big river's edge, singing an ancient song taught to him by his grandmother a long, long time ago:

Like the sun and the breeze, the Earth and the trees,
A raccoon's toughest job is simply to be;
Like the rain and the sky and the way the birds fly,
A raccoon's toughest job is simply to be.

Raccoon was busy licking excess dew from the long blades of grass when a bright orange butterfly fluttered past his nose, zigzagging this way and that. Raccoon could not resist. Quick as an arrow, he shot up after her, bursting with excitement. "I'll bet I can catch you, little butterfly!" he called out.

The little butterfly said, "I do not have time to play with you right now, Raccoon. I am busy looking for some nice flowers to land on," and she kept flitting along the way butterflies do, knowing, as did all the hard-working animals in the mountains, of Raccoon's reputation for wanting to play all the time and never get anything done. Meanwhile, Raccoon had been distracted by the invitation to wrestle with a hollow log. He and the log rolled out from a cloud of dust and skidded face first. It was a tie. Just then, he caught sight of the orange butterfly and began chasing her once again. He jumped high into the air as though he, too, could fly, flapping his little arms and legs with excitement.

Just as he was about to catch up with the little butterfly, Raccoon leapt high into the air and landed belly-first in the cold swirling waters of the river! *Splash!* "Help me! Help me!" he cried, kicking wildly about in the shallow waters. "I cannot swim!"

Doyi, Beaver, who was nearby, ignored Raccoon, knowing full well that raccoons can swim. Just like all the other animals, Beaver knew that Raccoon sometimes liked to play tricks on the other animals to get them to play, and he wasn't about to be fooled. Besides, he had too much to do before Iga-e-hinvdo, Grandfather Sun, dipped below the horizon.

Just then, Raccoon bumped up against one of the logs that held together Beaver's meager-looking dam. It was only partly finished and only partly impeded the river's flow, but it was well built. Raccoon opened his eyes once again and stopped splashing around in the water. There, on the far side of the dam, he could see that Beaver was still hard at work, just as he had been for the passing of several moons. The little orange butterfly was nowhere to be found. Raccoon rubbed the water out of his eyes and licked a little excess honey off his nose. Suddenly, he got an idea!

"Beaver," called out Raccoon, "your very majestic lodge has saved me from drowning in these waters, and I am grateful to you." Beaver nodded half-heartedly and continued his work of carefully positioning his freshly cut logs in just the right way.

"Beaver," called out Raccoon once again, "we must celebrate and give thanks to the Creator, for this is a great occasion deserving of some honey." Raccoon dragged his soaking, scrawny hide up onto the dam near the place where Beaver was working without hesitation. Raccoon began shaking his whole body furiously, spraying Beaver with excess water flying every which way. Beaver wiped his face off with one free hand, growling a little to himself.

"I know of a place," Raccoon continued loudly, waving his hands dramatically, as though speaking for all to hear, "where a very plump beehive hangs from a tree limb. I'll bet it is lonely, and we should probably visit with it for awhile. Not even Bear knows of this ripe place. All you would have to do, Brother, is chew the tree down and we could enjoy an afternoon snack to commemorate this occasion! Just think of that poor, plump beehive, hanging there all by itself. . . . Our brothers the bees have made too much of their delicious honey, and they would probably be more than grateful to us if we were to take a little of it off their hands."

Beaver said nothing and did not seem amused. Nevertheless, Raccoon continued with his eloquent speech: "Nearby, there is even a meadow covered with wildflowers of all colors where we can do a friendship dance when we're finished—just the two of us. . . . unless someone else wants to join in, of course."

Beaver continued laying logs and packing mud firmly into the crevices of his river lodge. "I do not have time to talk with you now, Raccoon," he chided. "You can see that I have work I must do."

Just beneath the sound of afternoon crickets and birds' singing and the occasional rustling of leaves, the river's water gurgled slowly, evenly. "Beaver, many moons have come and gone," pleaded Raccoon, "and none of them have seen you playing in the long grass as I do or watching with great wonder as Grandfather Sun drops below the horizon. You do not go searching for ripe berries or take long naps in Sun's warmth with your belly up."

"Winter is coming soon," replied Beaver, working tirelessly, "and you, Raccoon, will have no secure place to live."

Looking a bit puzzled as he watched Beaver laboring, Raccoon scrunched up his little black-and-white snout. "But Mother Earth always provides me with a place to live as long as I give thanks to her by appreciating all that she has to offer us and enjoying her great beauty."

"Raccoon, go and find someone else to play with," said Beaver, ". . . unless you want to hand me some of those logs over there." Raccoon shrugged his little shoulders. Then he plopped into the river head first and swam ashore downstream a little ways . . .

Many hours passed, and Beaver was still hard at work, just as he had been all day. He was concentrating so much on what he was doing that he didn't even notice the big dark clouds that had taken over the sky. He didn't even notice as the wind began picking up, and when the first hint of raindrops began to fall, Beaver just kept on working. He was determined to build his dam, and that was that.

"That silly old Raccoon," he muttered to himself, "thinking that I would just go off and leave my dam unfinished so that I could play with him." The raindrops were beginning to get bigger and fall more often now. Beaver wiped his forehead with a free hand and continued working as he talked to himself.

"I wonder what Raccoon is doing right now anyway. He's probably off somewhere trying to trick someone else into getting him some honey, or maybe he's picking flowers. That silly-willy." Beaver smiled a little to himself, then furrowed his brows once again and kept working.

The raindrops were falling even harder than before, and suddenly the thunder boomed with such loudness that it caught Beaver by surprise and sent him hurdling into the water with a great big splash! The river was starting to rise, and now the wind was blowing hard, too. All the trees were swaying to and fro as though they might jump right out of the ground, and the rain was pouring down so hard Beaver could barely see in front of himself. He swam as best he could back over to his dam and began to climb up on top of it. Just as he stood up and wiped the water out of his eyes, Beaver gasped at what he saw coming toward him. A flood! The river was crashing toward Beaver and his little dam with full force . . .

Not far away, Raccoon had taken shelter from the terrible storm in the hollow of a big old sycamore tree by the river. He was poking his little snout halfway out of the hollow so he could catch the delicious drops of rain falling from the huge sycamore leaves when he suddenly heard Beaver cry out, "Ahhhhh, help!!!"

Quickly, Raccoon scampered out of the hollow, squishing in the mud as he went. He knew Beaver was in trouble, and although Beaver never seemed to want to play, Raccoon knew that Beaver was his friend.

When Raccoon got to what was left of Beaver's dam, he could see that Beaver was caught between some of the logs and couldn't get free. Beaver needed help soon, or he would drown from the rushing waters.

"Beaver," cried Raccoon above the crashing of thunder and lightening, "I will get you free!" Beaver said nothing as he struggled not to swallow the water that was washing over him. The flooding waters had smashed Beaver's dam and everything else standing in its way. And now Beaver was in big trouble!

Using his sharp claws and strong arms and legs, Raccoon scooted carefully across one of the logs that was still firmly planted in the mud. When he got to where Beaver was stuck, he called out, "Beaver, grab hold of my tail and I will pull you free." Beaver did this, and, sure enough, Raccoon pulled him out from between the logs. Together, they scooted carefully back along the log until they got over to the river's edge. Then Raccoon led Beaver back to the safety of the old sycamore tree hollow where they could both stay safely until the storm let up. They had never seen a storm like this one before.

"Raccoon," said Beaver, breathing heavily, "you have saved my life, and I am grateful to you for this." Both of them were sopping wet and out of breath, and they looked scrawny with their fur matted against their bodies. Raccoon smiled at Beaver as he pulled some wild blackberries out of his special pouch and offered them to him. The berries were soaking wet, too, but somehow neither Beaver nor Raccoon cared. Together, they enjoyed a late afternoon snack, while the rain kept falling and the Red Thunder Beings continued beating their skydrum . . .

Since that time, Raccoon and Beaver have been the closest of friends, each one claiming the other as his "brother." Sometimes, if you go far enough back into the woods, you can hear the distant sounds of Raccoon and Beaver singing and dancing the Friendship Dance amid all the beautiful colors of the wildflowers and licking extra honey off their noses. And, sometimes, others do join in, and together they all dance in the afternoon warmth of Grandfather Sun, giving thanks for having someone to smile and play with.

And sometimes, just sometimes, if you go down to the river and look close enough, you will see a raccoon helping the beavers build their dams. And so, it is good.

....

BUSY BEAVER

Just as we were all once children, there is at least a little bit of Raccoon in all of us. As adults, however, many of us are renowned for our "busy beaver" phenomenon in which simply *being* is not enough. As adults, we learn of all the responsibilities required for us to live in the "real world." Hence, we seek to develop a "true purpose" in life, setting aside the carefree smile and wonder that Raccoon has for the world in order to construct our personal dams (which, oddly enough, never seem to be finished) wherein we seek that purpose. Some of us may have even accepted somewhere along the way the idea that we are only as worthwhile as the things we accomplish: the larger the dam, the "better" the person; the

more honest *work* that has been done, the greater the
reward, be it security, status, power, wealth, love, or anything
else. Still, one simple truth remains: We are not human
doings, we are human *beings*.

There is an implicit danger in sacrificing one's *being* for
the sake of *doing*. Sometimes, doing gives us a reason to
avoid being, to avoid our own inner experience. After all, a
human being's toughest job is simply to be, as Raccoon
might remind us. That is not to say that doing is not OK. It is
just as OK as being. Our challenge is to decide what is best
for us and where we can strike a balance between the two by
relating what we do to our inner experience and vice versa.

How often have you heard either yourself or someone
else saying, "I wish I had the time . . ." and yet you or they do
not *make* the time? They do not take the time to honor the
relationship between being and doing, and to actively learn
from it. Unfortunately, assuming that being and doing are
one and the same often proves harmful. Focusing on only
one in the belief that there is no distinction between the two
can lead to disharmony and feelings of emptiness or disconnectedness.

How often do strangers, upon meeting, inquire as to the
nature of one another's occupations or means of accomplishment as an indicator of status and relative worth? We
think that knowing what someone *does* for a living helps us
to gauge what kind of person someone *is*. Upon meeting
Raccoon, many of us might describe him as lazy and rather
irresponsible—we who stake our lives, the very value of our
life on this planet on doing. And what happens when we run
out of things to do? Well, this rarely happens. But when it
does? We just find more "things" to do! It's like drilling a hole

in water—only, in this case, we act as if the value of our existence depends upon whether or not we succeed in doing so.

Doing provides us with opportunities for learning. Hence, the old adage "If at first you don't succeed, try, try again." One gets the sense that it is really OK to be "beating your head against the wall" as long as you are doing *something*. There is a very important reason for doing; having things to do certainly can add purpose and direction to our lives. Yet having things to do can also take the discovery of meaning away. There is an old Indian saying that is relevant here: "If at first you don't think, and think again, don't bother trying."

Being says, "It's enough just to be; our purpose in life is to develop the inner self." Doing meanwhile advocates, "Be active; work hard, apply yourself fully, and your efforts will be rewarded." Walking in harmony and balance means experiencing both.

....

UNMASKING THAT FROM WITHIN

Traditionally, ceremonies were planned annually or even more frequently as ways of bringing people together for specific purposes in better understanding the relationship between being and doing. One form of ceremony practiced in many tribes involves the use of masks. The mask itself might be carved by the official mask maker in the tribe to describe a particular person as he or she was seen by the carver or the medicine man. Wearing the mask during ceremonial dance, then removing the mask, was powerful Medicine as one crossed worlds between that of the spirit and that of the physical. Mask wearers often represented a spirit being or sought to enlist the help of the spirits, asking the spirits to move through them.

The Iroquois, for instance, employed the mask for ceremonies in what was known as the False Face Society, whose duties included curing illness and keeping harmful Medicine at bay. Individuals became members of the False Face Society after receiving a vision that they were to do so. As members of this secret society, they conducted ceremonies while wearing masks that represented the spiritual agents whose responsibility it was to counteract harmful intentions.

The leader of the False Faces was said to be the Great World-Rim Dweller, who, closely associated with animals, controlled hunters' access to wild game based upon whether or not the proper hunting taboos were observed, apologies were made to the spirits of slain animals, and there was killing only out of need. For the Iroquois, there was an integral association between animals and disease that was mediated by the Great World-Rim Dweller, who had the ability to both cure illness and cause it. The performance of the False Faces led to the curing of illness and an eventual setting right of that which had been wronged.

The Cherokee made use of masks in a ceremony known as the Booger Dance, usually performed in late fall or winter. In this, a group of unidentified mask wearers disguised as "Boogers" entered domestic dwellings amidst a sequence of social and animal dances. The mask wearers, or Boogers, represented hideous ghosts or spirits that were thought to be responsible for illness or misfortune. The Boogers would dance in a circle, frightening children, making lewd gestures, and joking with adults, to whom they secretly disclosed their identities. One of the purposes of the Booger Dance, as a symbolic act of the communities, was a communal effort through parody to expel the disharmony introduced by disease or misfortune. Therefore, the Booger Dance served to bring the communities back into harmony and balance.

Thus, use of the mask traditionally allows certain persons to perform ceremonies necessary for the harmonious functioning of the community or tribe as a whole. The mask was further used by the Cherokee to emphasize the transitory nature of various social roles that people play, switching among them like masks deemed appropriate for certain situations and not for others. Following ceremonial participation in "doing," mask wearers often revealed their "true selves" by taking off their masks to just "be."

EXERCISE: Twelve Statements

Get a blank sheet of paper, and fill in the statement "I am _____" twelve times, writing down your responses as they come to you. What do you notice about the way that you responded? How many of the statements reflect *being*? How many of the statements reflect *doing*? Where do you place your own self-worth? Where do you see your own mindset being at this point in your life, and why? Where are you putting most of your time and energy? This has been another energy check.

··

LEARNING THE WAYS OF WATER

I remember my father telling me about an experience that he had with his grandfather that taught him the importance of being and doing. One day, my father was down by the riverside with his grandfather, learning the ways of

Mother Earth and all that she teaches us. He was observing carefully the ways being taught to him by his grandfather, although he was feeling a little overwhelmed since there was so much to learn, just as Mother Earth has so much to offer us.

His grandfather was giving thanks to the water when suddenly my father said to him, "Grandfather, I know that these ways are good and this is well . . . but if I went around giving thanks to everything that there is all the time, I would never get anything done."

The wise old man smiled as he continued and said, "That's right."

CHAPTER NINE

All in Good Time

*Great Spirit, you lived first, and you are older
than all need.*

—BLACK ELK, OGLALA LAKOTA MEDICINE MAN

S tillness is a pleasure. Let it become a pleasure *and* a privilege. And if in that stillness, you knew that tomorrow was your last day to be alive, what would today be like for you? Would you do anything differently? Would you see things any differently? How would you live your last day of life on Mother Earth? Let stillness become a friend and lifelong companion that you can turn to at any time.

We are mortal body, and we are immortal spirit. Our spirit chooses this body for all of its strengths and all of its limitations. We learn its strengths, and we learn to live with its limitations. Our spirit chooses this body—which is placed into the world within a particular set of circumstances at a particular point in time—to learn.

From Egela, Fire, we receive the heat that makes our hearts alive, pulsing with vitality and flickering with vibrance. From Elohino, Mother Earth, we receive the solid form of our physical being, that which we know as the body, made of all of the same substance that makes up every living thing in our world. From Ama, Water, we receive the life stream of our blood flowing ever outward before returning once again to the source of its beginning, only to flow again outward, giving life to the form. And from Unole, Wind, we receive our first breath of life and experience the Giveaway of our last sigh. This is the inner Circle of Life. This is why we give thanks always to the Four Directions, to that which makes us what we are, both in substance and in form.

And in the Center is our spirit, the ever-changing, everlasting connection with all that is, all that moves and flows and breathes and flickers. We are one with all that is, and all things are connected like the blood that unites one family. We arise, emerging from formlessness to separateness, and return once again to the formless, boundless, and undivided realm of the spirit—complete consciousness and forever emerging. We are our Nuwati, we learn our Nuwati, we become our Nuwati, and once again we are our Nuwati.

Years ago, physicists made an astonishing discovery exploring what is known as quantum theory. As they examined the subatomic world of atoms, the basic building blocks of all substance and form, they noticed that atoms consisted mainly of space in which infinitely tiny nuclei were orbited by other tiny particles, called electrons, bound to the nucleus by electromagnetic forces. Not only were these particles in a constant state of motion, but they also interacted with other particles in a never ending series of energy exchanges. Thus, rather than the particles being externally related to one another making the whole, they existed in a dynamic process of reciprocal interrelationships that are indistinguishable from the whole.

When physicists tried to examine light, which contains photons and other subatomic particles, they discovered that they could never establish both the location and momentum of a subatomic particle. One who wished to observe the location and momentum of an orbiting electron found that the very act of observation energized the electron, resulting in change of momentum or location. So they could locate the position of the electron but then not know its momentum, *or* they could determine the electron's momentum but not know its position. What made matters more complicated is that they discovered that all subatomic particles possess dual properties of being both substance *and* form! In other words, light, for example, could be seen as waves of energy *or* as particles in motion.

If the experiment were established to observe the nature of an electron as a wave, then it tended to behave like a wave. If the experiment were established to observe the nature of an electron as a particle, then it tended to behave like a particle. The Cartesian philosophy of duality, or dichotomy between observer (subject) and observed (object), broke down. (René Descartes was the seventeenth-century French philosopher who said that there is a separation between mind and matter, or between mind and body, which allowed scientists to treat matter as dead and completely separate from themselves; they therefore saw the material world as a multitude of different objects assembled into a huge machine. This philosophy popularized the belief that objective knowledge of the world could be acquired without the imposition of subjective values.)

Therefore, it was concluded that waves and particles are complementary in that they reflect different ways of describing the *same* reality. In fact, scientists found that with regard to the wave/particle duality, both modes of explanation are necessary if we are to achieve a complete understanding of the reality and nature of light. In essence, light is energy, no matter in what form you see it.

We, too, are energy, no matter in what form we see ourselves or others. Time gives us an abstract point of reference in which to locate ourselves. But spirit knows nothing of time, only growth . . .

SPENDING SOME TIME

So is now the right time? For what? For whatever. Many, many years ago, a man named Isaac Newton (who "discovered" gravity after having an apple fall on his head one day while he was sitting underneath an apple tree) asserted that time and space are absolute, highly deterministic, and provide an environment in which all motion in the material world takes place. The assumption was/is that time flows continuously and evenly on a "past–> present–> future" continuum that is linear and sequential in its progression.

Think about the way most of us live our lives. The North American ideal of "rugged individualism" has prescribed that life is similar to a ladder in which each rung should be seen as a progressive step toward increased separation or "separateness." Herein lies the true nature and reward of accomplishment. The toddler who learns to walk early is regarded as being more competent and independent, as well as having "a bright future." This is but one of a series of "steps" through which people proceed toward "individuality."

A gradual progression toward separateness takes place as we pass through several institutional rites of passage, including getting a driver's license, coming of age to vote, graduating from high school, going off to college, coming of age to consume alcohol, getting a job, and retiring, among others. In order to "be our own person," it is necessary that we "find ourselves" (as though self were something we had lost) by defining ourselves as a separate and distinct entity from that of "the crowd." Needless to say, "accomplishment" is the means through which this is achieved. Ironically, this constant struggle for separateness and distinction also leads to feelings of disconnectedness in many cases. *Doing* may or may not provide a safe haven in such instances.

For mainstream North American society, a person's worth is measured according to his or her accomplishments in life and potential and ambition for accomplishment. The more a person does, the more worthy that person is of respect and admiration. Think about what the following statement about our mainstream mentality embodies:

Since "nothing can stand in the way of progress,"
"the movers and shakers" are "in the fast lane" "on
their way to bigger and better things."

Unfortunately, this societal reverence for accomplishment is not of a cumulative nature, as is evidenced by the general devaluing of elders. Once people have grown older and spent their "potential," their perceived limited ability to be "productive" members of society marks them as somehow less than worthy. After all, "what are they good for" now? It becomes blatantly obvious that the emphasis falls more on the doing than on the person him- or herself. The absence of doing usually implies some form of personal inadequacy, as seen with the mainstream views and treatment of elders.

So-called inactivity is abhorred in this society, which remarks, "If you don't know what to do, at least *do some-thing!*" This is the same mainstream culture that worships time as a resource to be utilized for the sake of action. Time is an abstract concept reflecting a mechanistic worldview for the purpose of guiding human interaction and providing a more precise scientific measurement of life. It has thus become tangible to us (reminiscent of Frankenstein's monster brought to life), and it has now achieved the ability to control our lives instead. Think about all of the things that we do with this precious commodity:

> We *have* time.
> We *give* time.
> We *gain* time.
> We *lose* time.
> We *find* time.
> We *use* time.
> We *donate* time.
> We *plan* time.
> We *make* time.
> We *take* time.
> We *buy* time.
> We *save* time.
> We *spend* time.
> We *waste* time.
> We *borrow* time.

We *budget* time.
We *invest* time.
We *manage* time.
We *wait for* time.
We *look for* time.
We *search for* time.
We *pray for* time.
We *watch* time.

Always, at the heart of it all, we are using time to *do* things. However, when there is nothing more to do, then time becomes a burden to us, and in the end

We *kill* time.

So who is right, Beaver or Raccoon? Maybe they are both right. It is really no one's place to say whether we should slave away building dams or run around frolicking like raccoons. However, each of us in our search for whatever it is that we seek has the ability to temper one with the other—Beaver *and* Raccoon, doing *and* being. And what is the lesson of being or the lesson of doing? That is for you to find out.

....

THE FOURTH DIMENSION

What do you think it would be like if we lived in a timeless dimension—in other words, if time did not exist and we therefore never had to worry about time? What would life be like?

Time contributes to memory (past) and expectation (future)—two of the things in life that can truly make us who we are and that also can bind us, preventing us from being who we could be. When we are born, we enter the world and are connected to time—if nothing else, through the natural processes of our physical body. When we cross over ("die"), we are released from the grips of time into the timeless world of spirit. In between those two events, we live our lives, always limited at any given point in time to what we are able to perceive from our current frame of reference. Remove the restraint of time, and there would be no anxiety about beginning or about goals/outcome. There would be no fear of death, or ending.

We live in a world that (supposedly) consists of three dimensions. The fourth dimension is time. Everything that exists within the first three dimensions moves and changes along the fourth dimension of time. Take that away, and what would be left of the other three dimensions? You have just glimpsed the spirit world. You will again—don't worry. In the meantime, step into the flow . . .

RESONANCE AND DISSONANCE

When was the last time you heard a really good song and just had to stop everything else and maybe dance, or sing, or just listen to it? Maybe it was a song that really touched you and sent a chill down your spine or put butterflies in your stomach, or maybe it was a song that just downright made you feel good. Maybe it was a song that had a lot of memories for you and took you back to that time. Maybe it was a song that you knew you had heard somewhere before, but never could quite place it. Maybe it was a song that you had never heard before, but somehow it really resonated with your spirit. Maybe it was a song that was just in your mind;

maybe you weren't even all that conscious of it or didn't realize that you were humming it silently to yourself (or singing it
out loud, for those of you who are more extraverted).

Why do certain songs feel really good to you, others really rub you the wrong way, and still others leave you feeling
indifferent? Incidentally, have you ever noticed how people,
when keeping rhythmic time to music, tend to clap on beats
two and four, while tapping their feet on beats one and
three? (Go ahead—try it!) It is a matter of resonance and dissonance. The feet are grounded (one and three), the hands
reach for the sky (two and four). It is a matter of harmony
and balance.

People will say to me, "So how did you make up your
mind about that . . ." and I sometimes say, "I don't know—it
just felt good to me." I know when something really resonates with me. I know when something causes dissonance
for me. I know when I am indifferent to something. If I pay
close attention to my own inner reactions to things, places,
and people, I learn a lot about those things, places, and people, and I learn a lot about myself and my own Medicine.
How about you? The same? I don't know about you, but I try
to seek out those things, places, and people that resonate
with me.

So do opposites attract, or does like attract like (more
popularly phrased as, birds of a feather flock together)?
Magnets show us some truth in this. If we take two magnets,
put them facing one another and they stick to one another,
then they are resonating with one another. However, if we
take the same two magnets but turn one of them around so
that the opposite side is showing, the two magnets will repel
one another with all of their might. That is because there is a

dissonance in the energy between the two by the very nature of what they are, even though they are the same two magnets.

What is my point? Simple. Step away from linear time and tune into the natural rhythms that are all around you and within you. Seek out those things, places, and people that resonate with you and with which/whom you resonate. And the next time someone says to you, "How did you make up your mind about that?" just tell them, "I don't know, I guess it really resonated with me . . ."

Some things, places, and people are a lot like a good song, you know.

EXERCISE: A Little Music Makes the Medicine Go Down

As you think about the things, places, and people that resonate with you at this point in your life, why not try putting that energy to music? You might begin by allowing a special melody to come to you. Or you may just want to start talking it out. It doesn't have to be fancy—in fact, the simpler the better. But it must have power for you. Before you know it, you will have created a song or chant that captures the Medicine of whatever feeling, image, or experience you are drawing from.

This becomes a medicine chant for you and one that holds a great deal of personal power, not only because it resonates with you, but because it *is* you. Your medicine chant can bring you back to that energy from which it originated any time. It may offer you comfort in times of hardship or sadness. It may serve as a way to celebrate good times or good feelings. It may be your way of offering your prayers of thankfulness for all of the gifts that you have received. And so, it is good.

Here is an example of a Cherokee chant that gives thanks to the four winds for carrying our prayers where they need to go:

Clearing Way Song

U-no-le-huh u-no-le
U-no-le-huh u-no-le
U-no-le-hey u-no-le
U-no-le-hey u-no-le

U-no-le-huh u-no-le
U-no-le-huh u-no-le
U-no-le-hey u-no-le
U-no-le-hey u-no-le
(x 4)

O-ge-do-da u-no-le
O-ge-do-da u-no-le
U-no-le-hey u-no-le
U-no-le-hey u-no-le

U-no-le-huh u-no-le
U-no-le-huh u-no-le
U-no-le-hey u-no-le
U-no-le-hey u-no-le
(x 3)

....

TIME ENOUGH

So if you knew that today was your last day of life on Mother Earth, how would you spend your time? Where would you go; who would you see? What would you want to feel? What would you want to experience? Would you do anything differently? Would you see things any differently? What would you remember? Would it have all been worthwhile?

CHAPTER TEN

Keeping It All Balanced

The Earth has received the embraces of the Sun, and
we shall see the results of that love!
—SITTING BULL, HUNKPAPA LAKOTA CHIEF

If you know that you have limited energy and you know that you are here for a limited amount of time, how will you use the energy that you have, as well as the energy that you receive? How will you maintain your energy, and how will you replenish it? How will you express gratefulness for the many good things that have come your way? What will you do with the gift of life that you carry in your body?

In the Medicine Way, giving and receiving energy occurs in all four dimensions of the inner life circle, including spirit, natural environment, mind, and body. Whatever affects one, affects all. Therefore, as we think about wellness and healing through harmony and balance, we seek to bring the dimensions of the life circle together into a unified, purposeful whole. In Cherokee tradition, we always begin in the East with spiritual Medicine, then in the South with natural Medicine, then the West with physical Medicine, and finally, the North with mental Medicine. These four dimensions, like opposites, exist as extensions of each other in helping us discover and offer our sacred gifts.

....

SPIRITUAL MEDICINE

Tapping the Well

Finding your Medicine means tapping into your own intuitive energy and listening to it. All too often, we are taught to think and not to feel, when in fact we can do both, and in doing so, we open ourselves up to our own inner wisdom. There is much sacred wisdom available to us if we learn how to recognize what is good for us, then open up and make ourselves available to it.

Healing Ways

As you come into your own Medicine, you are discovering your own personal way of being a helper to all our relations. You are learning about yourself, about the gift of life, and about the best way to utilize this sacred gift. What are the things that are important to you? What are your strengths? Your limitations? What holds power for you? What are the objects that hold Medicine for you? What are some special gifts you've received from others? How can you use these? How can you learn from these? What are the ceremonies that hold Medicine for you? And how can they best help you on your path? Are there other things you would like to include or learn more about? In addition, as was mentioned earlier, pay attention to your dreams. These are ways of communicating with yourself, with others, and of being communicated with. They can offer valuable lessons or resolutions.

Laughing It Up

Many people hold the expectation that in order for an experience to be considered "spiritual," it must be serious, intense, and deeply profound. Those are not my thoughts exactly: Some of the most spiritual experiences I have ever had include those times when I have nearly choked from laughing so hard. Moreover, some of the most spiritual people I have ever known are those who know how to laugh, don't always take everything (including themselves) so seriously, and know how to relate to others through laughter as well. (Connect.) You see, when something has become *so* serious and *so* sacred that we cannot laugh about it or ourselves, then that something has lost its true sacredness. We lose sight of what is truly sacred. It becomes distant, elevated, untouchable. (Disconnect.)

Each day, make it a point to find something to laugh about. If nothing comes up, make something humorous happen, and if possible, always try to share these moments with someone else. Look for the joy in life. This is when you truly begin to grasp the life energy of things around you and make yourself available to that which transcends physical form. Needless to say, people who are able to laugh are usually the same ones who are able to overcome moments of discouragement and disappointment by taking stock and utilizing what they do have. As George Goodstriker, Blackfoot, has said, "Humor is the WD-40 of healing" (Wilson Schaef, *Native Wisdom for White Minds*, May 5).

....

NATURAL MEDICINE

Due to selective perception, we tend to miss a great deal of what occurs around us. In this world, there is so much to take in that we tend to selectively notice certain things and disregard other things, especially if they do not have any direct bearing on us. This is so that we don't become overwhelmed with too much information. This is also because we learn to make value judgments that certain things are important and other things are less important. This helps us make decisions on a daily basis. It also creates the limits of our awareness. Therefore, we need to teach ourselves to experience not only through the mind, but through the senses.

Opening up to the universe means "feeling" life as it happens all around us and through us. This creates a sense of awareness, intuition, and calm. It allows us to recognize and use energy. Everything has energy. Example: Place the palms of your hands opposite one another and slowly move them toward each other. Feel the energy. Move your hands back and forth. Feel a sense of tingling or gentle tension like two magnets repelling one another. That is life energy. Opening up to the Nuwati means that we have to do things in life because we want to, because we enjoy what we are doing, and we believe in them. That is the point of the Circle of Life and the many paths that we are all walking.

Soon we see things that we have not seen before or see things in a way that we have not seen them before. And soon we are able to hear the little plants talking to us once again, telling us how to use their Medicine.

....

PHYSICAL MEDICINE

Eating Well

These days, it is not surprising to find that a great deal of the illness and chronic health problems many people are experiencing is due to poor nutrition and eating habits. In the old days, Indian people ate what Mother Earth offered them naturally, such as wild greens and vegetables (corn, beans, squash); roots, herbs, berries, fruits, and honey; and wild meat or fish. The delicate balance maintained within the body resembled the natural balance that existed outside of the body in the natural surroundings. Today, there are so many different foods (not always rich with quality nutrients) available to us that we must choose wisely what goes into our bodies in order to maintain our physical balance. The following foods and supplements promote the natural balance that is required for the body to function normally and healthfully:

- water (purified)
- raw fruits and vegetables
- whole grains and complex carbohydrates
- meat (buy chemical-free meat; eat more chicken and fish than red meat; substitute other proteins for meat sometimes)
- vitamins (supplementing whatever may be lacking in your diet)

Certain foods and substances tax or interfere with the body's normal process of taking in nutrients and eliminating wastes or toxins from the system. These can cause a buildup of toxins in the system that can result in illness, when the

body's normal ability to eliminate them becomes overwhelmed. Foods and substances to stay away from or take in
moderation include the following:

- caffeine
- salt
- sugars
- saccharin
- red meat
- animal skins
- fats
- oils
- alcohol
- processed foods
- preservatives
- chemicals in food

Getting Some Air and Having a Good Sweat
 Any form of exercise that gives the body a chance to
strengthen its cardiovascular system and muscles as well as
eliminate toxins from the bloodstream through the natural
process of sweating holds many healthy benefits. Moreover,
when we are feeling bad, angry, frustrated, or low on energy,
or when we feel pressured or cannot relate well to the people
around us, exercising can offer a perfect solution. It is difficult to feel negative while our blood is pumping fresh oxygen
through our body and we see the beauty of Mother Earth all
around us.

And don't forget to stretch. It is a good idea to stretch
both before and after exercise to maintain muscle flexibility
and prevent injury. In fact, it is not a bad idea to stretch each
morning before you begin your day and in the evening before

you go to bed. (Hold each position for thirty seconds; don't bounce; breath slowly, deeply, and regularly.)

Sexuality and Sensuality

Got your attention, didn't I? Good, I am glad you are paying attention . . . to life that is. An important part of experiencing our physical selves is enjoying our sensuality—the expression of our loving, sexual being. This is an important way of sharing with another special person and enjoying life energy together. This is a natural way of celebrating the life energy that makes up the entire universe. Open up to all of your senses and explore the feelings that happen within you. Experience the sense of joy, relaxation, and wonder, and share this with another.

....

MENTAL MEDICINE

Clarity of Thought Brings Clarity of Action

Each of us has what is called a "shock organ." This is a particular organ, system, or area of the body to which we send the stress, anxiety, fear, and pain that come from what we experience in life. The shock organ or area varies from person to person; it might be the neck and shoulders, the head, the throat, the heart, the stomach or intestines, and so on. Thus, for many of us, when we get ourselves out of balance, the first thing to go is the shock organ. However, many traditional healers function from the belief that illness is not simply a physical malfunction, but rather a combined holistic response to disharmony and imbalance. As such, a person's shock organ represents a greater symbolic lesson and meaning for that particular person.

The lesson? Learn how to release, how to create, how to

live. Be honest with yourself and with others. Participate in
your ceremonies and quiet time. Express yourself through
creative outlets such as painting, sewing, drawing, acting,
singing, dancing, exercising, writing, or other things that
allow you to express your true self (beading, pottery, wood-
working, leatherworking, and other crafts were traditional
ways of relaxing, releasing, and praying).

What is it that *moves* you? Never do something just to be
doing it; do it because you *feel* it! Make a list of the things
that make you happy; ask others what makes them happy.
Strive for balance of spirituality, creativity, work, enjoyment,
exercise, diet, and self-awareness. As always, it is important
to utilize what we have available to us in our lives and to be
thankful for it. This brings clarity of mind that flows into all
other aspects of our lives.

Finding Your Own Vision

Many people live out their lives doing what they think
they *should* be doing and not necessarily doing what they
want to be doing. For some, this is OK, and for others, it is
miserable. And it is also scary to venture into the unknown
territory. But in the Medicine, accepting someone else's
vision is having no vision at all. There is an old saying, "Take
everything in the palms of your hands and see what's worth
keeping, then blow the rest away with a breath of kindness."
Hold onto what works, and throw out what does not work
for you. Enjoy every day of life that you have been given, and
be thankful for it. Even the most dire circumstances cannot
sway one who sees clearly and follows his or her inner vision
with every bit of spirit. As Sequichie Comingdeer, Cherokee,
has said, "The death of fear is in doing what you fear to do."
Spread your wings and . . .

Francene Hart

CHAPTER ELEVEN

Crossing the Bridge

*I'm the spirit's janitor. All I do is wipe the windows a
little bit so you can see out for yourself.*

—GODFREY CHIPS, LAKOTA MEDICINE MAN

O nce, when I was teaching a class on multicultural
counseling, I stood before the group of peering
eyes and asked my students, "What is it that you see
when you look at me?" They responded by telling me that
they saw many different things. They saw a male who was tall
and thin. They saw a person with brown eyes, long hair, and
a quiet way. They saw someone who liked working with people, someone who was "laid back," someone who was Indian
and White. They saw someone who was "full of it" (my
words, not theirs; I think they said something like "a person
who knows a lot of things"). They said that they saw much by
looking at me.

I told them that what they saw before them was one of the

many places where the four winds meet. I told them that what they saw when they looked at me was all of my family and anyone who had ever offered help to me or my family for all of the generations of time that have ever existed. I told them that what they saw was all of the Garretts who had ever lived, all of the Riters who had ever lived, all of the Millers and Youtz, all of the Rogers, Walkingsticks (Tlanusta), Crisps, Warrens, Kings, and Paynes who had ever lived on Mother Earth. I am the place where they all meet. I am the bridge from one generation to the next, the culmination of all of the experiences of all of the people who are my ancestors and relatives, both in blood and spirit. The spirit never dies.

There was also another time when, after I had given a professional presentation on counseling Native Americans, a man came up to me with a puzzled look on his face. I thought maybe I had been unclear in my presentation of some of the material. I could tell that his wheels were turning. He said to me, "I guess what I don't understand is, are you Indian or are you White?" From some of my brief description of my background and family heritage, he had concretely (and quite innocently) calculated up in his mind what he believed my blood quantum to be. I told him gently, "I am both." The spirit never dies.

As one Cherokee elder put it, "Plants know that they can't grow if they don't know their roots and can't draw from the source of it all." And so, as I talk about the Medicine, I must allow you to look into the relation from one generation to the next. I must show you a picture of the bridge and let you feel what it is like to walk across it, from one world to another.

I have always been interested in my father's journey as a medicine teacher and as a person. To me, his life has always been symbolic of what it means to seek our balance and use our gifts. He has always had many special gifts from the time that he was very young, but he had to learn what they were and what to do with them—just like any of us in life. Harmony and balance is not a point that you eventually reach and then have to figure out a way to stay there; it is a constant state of living and learning—with clarity and compassion. As we are seeking our own harmony and balance, we are seeking our vision. We are seeking to walk upon the wind and let it carry us where we need to be and show us what we in our hearts understand already.

As a boy I wondered, *Where exactly do the sky and Earth meet?* I remember hearing stories about that "in-between" time of day becoming night (dusk) or night becoming day (dawn), and how much the spirits like to dance during that time. I could be seen squinting at dawn or dusk, trying to catch a glimpse of the spirit people dancing. I could be found frozen still, listening intently for the sound of their footsteps. In our lives, we cross many bridges, and eventually, we cross the bridge between the physical and spirit worlds as we continue our journey. Thus, we must understand truly where we have come from, where we are, and where we are going. When we have peace with this journey and are able to see beauty in all things, then we are walking the path of Good Medicine.

When you listen to the story of a person's life, you glimpse their essence, as well as learning about life and about your own Medicine. One gentle spring day in 1995, I sat down with my father, J.T. Garrett, and asked him to tell me the story of his life. The following sections paint a picture of the wisdom he shared. And so, it is good.

....

WHAT IS IN A NAME

In the traditional way, one of the first ways that you learn to identify yourself and your own inner power in relation to those around you is through your name. Often, you are given an "official" name, a nickname (as earned), and an Indian name (which is very sacred, and usually not shared with many people). Something as simple as a name holds Medicine:

> My mother used to call me Jaybird, but she never really said it in front of anybody else; she would always just say that to me. She'd tell me that Grandpa [her father, Oscar Walkingstick Rogers] always had pet names for everybody. Later on, I realized that that was just the way Indians do: everybody has a name based on how they behave or some incident that's occurred. I was usually called J.T. and I really didn't like it, but I didn't want to be called Jasper, which was my first name. During World War II, my father, who was Jasper Sr., was called "Jap" for short. At that time nobody wanted to be called that, and I didn't want to be called "little Jap." My mother knew all that and so she would call me Jaybird or something that was Indian.

....

YOU GOTTA UNDERSTAND THE STORIES

In the Medicine, life and particular ways of doing things are not explained in a textbook manner to help people master certain objectives through the acquisition of knowledge.

Stories are told subtly as a way of relating the essence of life through an experience or legend upon which the listener is invited to reflect and from which to choose his or her own lessons or meaning. There is always respect for choice. Moreover, the stories allow the listener to train his or her mind in the ability to see things in pictures and to see beyond the surface of the immediate. The Medicine Way demonstrates respect for where each person is in his or her own journey, and the stories show us an image of where we come from, which has brought us to where we are now.

She [Dad's mother, Ruth Rogers Garrett] would tell me stories about my family and stories of the "Removal." It was after World War II, and even very young I remember some of the Japanese Americans being removed from their homes and put into camps. So I had this picture in my mind, when my mother would talk about the Indian Removal, of Indians being moved from their homes and put in these barricade camps. And she would say that they were rounded up from Red Clay country [northern Georgia] and over into Tennessee and around Sevierville and all the way up to Big Cove and in the mountains all the way up to the West Virginia and Tennessee lines—even down to South Carolina and North Carolina—and put in these barricades.

So I had this picture in my mind of all these Indians looking like Japanese, and they were all put in these barricades and just kept there. But also in my mind, maybe because of the newsreels I would see each Saturday when we would go to the movies, the Japanese all got out eventually, so as my mother would tell the story, I just assumed that all the Indians got out, too.

And when my mother would tell me about the Indian Removal, she'd tell me about a great, great, great grandma—her name was Chenowah and she was from the Walkingstick family. It would have been in 1838 that she would have been transported or moved or marched, or however they made people go—by wagon, by horse, whatever you had—to west of the Mississippi under what they called the Indian Removal Act. My mother told me that Chenowah was an old lady. I have no idea how old, but I had a picture in my mind of this old lady with this blanket on and a scarf on her head, walking all the way back from Oklahoma after the Removal, because once the government got all the Indian people there, there was no control to keep them there. And so many of them just went different places.

That's the reason that some of the families are located in Texas and all the way back to West Virginia, 'cause they couldn't go back to where they thought their home was. They were told that their homes were sold under treaty and they had no homes left, so a lot of them scattered all over the place.

I think the stories probably gave me a sense of connection with the Indian side [of his heritage] more than anything else. What I remember most of all is everything my grandfather, Oscar Walkingstick Rogers, ever said to me. He must have been the tallest man in the world. I was such a little boy, and I'd look up at him and he was tall—tall and slender. Boy, I thought he was such a fine man.

The first thing he'd say every time I'd see him was "Ceo Tsayoga," in other words, "Hello there, little bird—how're you doing?" The first thing he would always do is put me up on his shoulders, and take me down to the creek bank. He'd say, "Come on, let's go to the creek bank . . . gonna do some fishin'."

But I never fished—I never got a chance to fish. It's like if he had a chance to take me fishing, that was a chance to tell me stories, teach me values. We never brought home any fish. I think he would always put the fish back, even if he caught one.

But I remember one time when I was a little guy, we were down on the creek bank, and he said, "Put your feet in the water—you know, it's healing. The energy of the water will just come right on up your body and it'll say, 'Oooh'—just makes you feel so good." He said, "Let me put my feet in the water," and I remember he had *big* long feet. I remember him sticking those big long feet in the water and the fish would all take off, and he'd say, "That's because my feet stink—I got stinky feet." I remember little things like that.

But one time I had my feet in the water—my grandfather was sitting on a rock—and a little old piece of wood came down and hit me, and man, I jumped up real fast! "What was that?" I asked. And he said, "Oh, it was probably one of them water dogs." And I said, "Do what?" "Yeah," he said, "got big ol' water dogs that come down through here. You gotta be careful, 'cause every once in awhile, they just reach up and grab you. . . . See, if you don't hear them barking, you don't know they're there."

So I had this picture of something that was roaming around in the water called a "water dog," going "rooh, rooh, rooh, rooh," and I kept listening to see if I'd hear them barking. I don't know that I ever understood what a water dog was, but he used to tell me they were there, and I believed everything he said. Even to this day, when I go down to the creek bank, every once in awhile I'll just kind of listen to see if I hear any water dogs barking. But I'm sure it was a stick that was just going down through the current.

One day my grandfather, my uncle, and I were sitting together, and there was this little chickadee. My grandfather would say, "Chick-a-dee, chick-a-dee, won't you come here and play with me?" The little bird kept flopping around with its little legs. He'd look, walk around a little, then look, then go away and come back, look . . .

And then I saw this little earthworm—it was *real small*. And it was kind of squiggling around, moving around in the earth. It would come up a little bit, then it would go back down and come back up. And I realized that the little bird was looking at that worm. I had this picture of the little worm coming up and saying, "Ah, this looks pretty good. Well, I'd better go back down and do my earth work."

I said to my grandfather, "What's the little earthworm doing?" He said, "Well, you gotta understand the story of the little earthworm. In the beginning of time, after the big buzzard came down and messed up the land, it dried up—the ground was hard. The earth said, 'Whoa, I'm so hard and cracked; I'm hurt all over.'

"The Great One said, 'Well, we'll put some little helpers there to loosen up your soil. Besides, the plants won't grow on soil that's not loose, and the water will just run off.' So the Great One sent the little earthworm."

That earthworm was a little playful thing. He liked to get in the earth and move around, and *swzzeeet*, take the soil inside of him. (Grandfather used to say, "You know, they're good to eat, too. The sand's not good, but you can cut 'em open and cook 'em up—it's good protein." And I would think, *Yuuuck*—you know, imagine eating an earthworm.)

So this little earthworm would just kind of look up and say, "Oooh, it's a pretty day," and then he'd squiggle down in the earth again. I saw this little bird go over there and, *SHHHPP*, he grabbed that earthworm. And I could almost hear in my mind this little earthworm saying, "Oh, no! Wait a minute, wait a minute! You don't want to pull me out of the earth," because the bird was trying to pull and the earthworm was trying to go back down in the dirt. He had a time pulling that worm out of the ground, but sure enough, he got it up, and it was flipping around.

And I had this image: I could hear the earthworm saying, "Wait a minute—you don't want *me* because I have a purpose here. If you take me away, I won't be able to do what I'm put here to do—the Great One gave me a job to do."

And I could almost hear the little bird saying, "No, I'm hungry, and I'm gonna EAT YOU UP."

The earthworm said, "Yeah, but if you eat me, then I won't be able to loosen up the ground . . ."

According to my grandfather, the very first earthworms were put here to loosen up the ground so that the sunflower seeds would grow—a garden could never start unless the sunflower seeds were planted. The *big* sunflower plants could look up into the sky and give thanks to Grandfather Sun and keep a watch on all the plants, keeping all the birds and animals from coming in—the sunflower had a purpose.

Anyway, I could see this little earthworm saying, "Please, don't take me—I've gotta do my job," and the next thing I knew, *GUULLP*! Then the chickadee just flew off. Part of that worm went in his mouth, and I could still see it moving around.

Another thing that I remember is that Grandpa Oscar

Walkingstick Rogers kind of liked pretty girls, but he wouldn't look at them too much. He'd look down, then glance over and look just a little bit. And he'd say, "There's a certain way to look at a pretty woman." Boy, I wanted to know how to do that 'cause I didn't want to get myself in trouble!

One time, I saw this pretty woman and I was kind of looking. He said, "Kind of like her, eh?" I said, "Oh no, Sir, I'm not looking at–at what you think I'm looking at . . ." And he said, "Well, I'm not looking either. That's the reason I look down, and I just take a glance over–see."

The reason that was special to me was because he said, "I just take a glance, and I keep it in my mind." I thought, *Well, I've gotta keep it in my mind, too.* So it became real important for me to keep things in my mind. So I'd draw pictures–I used to draw a lot when I was real young. Because I knew that I couldn't remember all the plants I used to see, I'd draw pictures of them. I learned a lot about plants; they always seemed to be an influence in my life.

....

SEEKING THE WAY THAT IS NATURAL

The actual medicinal or biochemical part of medicine used for healing purposes, as with herbal remedies, is only a small part of the Medicine. There is a power in every living thing that must be listened to and understood. Thus, seeking the natural way also means seeking the mental, physical, and spiritual ways as well.

At an early age, I learned to know how to take care of myself in natural ways and to seek natural ways. Every time we'd go to the mountains, Aunt Shirley would take me out and show me different plants. I seemed to have a green thumb. My very first job—I believe I was eleven or twelve at the time—was taking care of a man's garden. He was a very wealthy man, and he had this large garden with a lot of flowers. So I became influenced by plants and flowers; it just seemed like I had a natural knowledge of how to work with plants. I seemed to communicate with them, but I never told anybody, 'cause that wasn't cool. You don't want to say, "Hey, Daddio, I've been out talking to some plants," or somebody would think you were a looney tune.

Another time I remember being influenced by plants was the one time I had an earache. I was hurting and holding my ear, and my uncle Charles said, "What's going on there?"

I said, "Well, I've got an earache."

He said, "Shoot, that's no problem. What did your momma do for you?"

I said, "Momma's not around, and Grandma's cooking." She was a short order cook. Everybody worked doing something so they could bring an income into the family.

"Ah, it's no problem," he said. "Let's find one of those puffballs."

"What?" I said.

"You know—a puffball," he said. "You ever stepped on one of those things, and they go *pweeskhkt*? It's a little brown thing on the ground in the woods."

And sure enough, we went into the woods and there were these little brown things. He just opened one up and took that stuff and put it down in my ear. Needless to say, I didn't have any idea that the puffball had antibacterial properties, but that's basically what it was. Uncle Charles said, "If we had some distilled water, we could put it in some, but you don't want to use this [puddle] water 'cause it's got all that *stuff* in it. You don't want to put anything like that in your ear—it'll just make it worse."

I always used to drink tea as well. We didn't have tea bags; we used to get tea in bulk. And you would make your own bag. There was a certain cloth my grandma would buy. We would just cut it up and tie it up to make our own tea bags, and then we would mix up whatever we wanted to. As an example, if I had a sore throat or a cough, Grandma would get some black cherry or wild cherry bark, and she'd mix it up with some plantain leaf. She'd steep that, and that's what we would take. I was influenced by all these things.

....

IT'S NOT THE MEDICINE THAT DOES THE WORK

In Cherokee teachings, there is a big difference between "medicine" (cure) and the "Medicine" (essence). One of the teachings of the Medicine, especially with regard to the use of natural remedies, is that it is not just the medicine of the plant that creates healing within the body, but the relationship of the recipient with that plant and the relationship of the healer with that plant that creates healing in the spirit (Medicine). Thus, it is the energy of these very sacred relationships that creates healing, as well as a reverence for the "natural way of things" (Rule of Acceptance), knowing that everything has its purpose and its own time.

Well, my grandfather passed on; he died of cancer. And that's something that really bothered me because I couldn't understand, if he was such a powerful medicine man, such a powerful spiritual man, why he had to die. Why didn't he have Medicine to cure himself? He had told me, "There's a plant and there's Medicine for everything. Anything that ever happens to you in your life, there's always a special plant out there for it—all you have to do is go out and seek it, and let it find you."

So when my grandfather died, I kept thinking, *Why didn't he seek it?* I guess that was the first time I realized that people die anyway. That was a concept that I couldn't understand. If we've got Medicine, why were people dying? Keep in mind, that was a period of time when a lot of people would die every year because of influenza—flu. That was also a time when there were diseases like polio; in fact, a good friend of mine got polio. And I couldn't understand why it happened if we had all this Medicine. I remember asking one of my uncles, Tingaling Walkingstick Rogers, "Why didn't he find his own Medicine?"

Uncle Tingaling went through the Bataan Death March during World War II; he was a decorated soldier like many of my uncles who were in the war at that time. Tingaling had pretty much survived on what he could find. He knew plants. He knew how to prepare them, how to fix them, how to cook them, and how to use them for medicine. And he told me a number of times that that's what helped him to survive.

Uncle Ting would always volunteer for detail to go out and work in the hardest, hottest, worst jobs digging up plants and cutting up logs, 'cause he'd scrape part of the bark off the trees for medicine. And he'd know what the plant could be used for by something that he called "similars." Even to this day, the Cherokee feel that there's a "similar" plant for everything that ails you. If it's your heart, it'll be shaped like a heart leaf; if it's your liver, it'll be shaped like a spade—things like that.

Uncle Ting told me, "One thing you have to learn is that when it's somebody's time—and everybody has their own time—it's not the medicine that does the work, it's the person who has to do the work. It's true even with Medicine—you have to seek your own Medicine."

....

CROSSING OVER

In the Medicine Way, "crossing over" refers to the literal or symbolic process of being able to move between worlds—for example, between the physical world and the spirit world. Or it may be moving from one state of consciousness to another as a form of shifting for a particular purpose (i.e., healing) and then returning to the original state. Those who are chosen by the spirits to become medicine persons often go through a symbolic process of death and rebirth as a ceremonial way of "crossing over" into a state of receptivity that allows them to work with the Medicine. For many, this is a process that takes a lifetime.

When I would go back to the reservation [they lived in Florida for awhile where there was work], I would think to myself, *Boy they're really out of touch; like they're not cool, man. Gotta go back to Fernandina where things are happenin'*. We were very much influenced by Black music back then. At that time, it was called rhythm and blues. And so, unlike my friends in the mountains who were into country or rockabilly, I was into rhythm and blues. I used to enjoy listening to a lot of it 'cause they sang about something from the soul, something from the heart and spirit. But I never put any of that together.

My dad decided to sell his business. He decided that it was time for us to move back to the mountains. I was, by that time, a senior in high school, and leaving all my friends and my girlfriend was pretty traumatic. But when we went to the mountains, it was like going into a fairy land; I don't know how to describe it otherwise. The feeling I had was almost as though the real world was out there, in Fernandina, and I was going into this magic land.

I was there about six months when I ran into a lady by the name of Mary. And she said that the medicine man wanted to see me; he knew that I was Oscar's boy—his grandson. Now, I had no idea who the medicine man was. I had an image of this old guy sitting there with long gray hair. Maybe I was pretty much influenced by the cowboy and Indian era, too. The Indians wouldn't say much—they weren't too bright as portrayed in the pictures. And the cowboys had all the answers. Well, lo and behold, I did finally realize that the cowboys didn't know as much as I thought, compared with another kind of knowledge and understanding that I was suddenly faced with.

When I first met the medicine man, I just saw him from a distance; that's as far as I was supposed to get. He just wanted to see me. I thought that was strange. Then maybe the second time or third time, even though he still wouldn't talk to me, I remember him saying, "Yep, that's Oscar's boy—no question about it." Then it was like I was OK. But I also remember him saying, "Boy, he sure is White."

Now what was strange about that was that I used to tan real easily, and I stayed dark all the time—in Fernandina, they would make comments about me being a renegade Indian.

And I thought, *Wow, I look White—gee, I've even got a sun tan.* But you'd have to see this old man—he was really dark. He had that dark black hair.

Then one day Aunt Shirley introduced me to another "old man." Actually he was in his mid-fifties, but I thought he was old. Now *I'm* fifty-two; I'm as old as he was then. She told me he knew a lot about plants. It was almost as though my whole world shifted. What I had thought was really important before didn't mean a thing to me anymore. I don't even remember writing that many letters to my friends 'cause it didn't make any difference—now I had this exciting new world.

Then I went to college. I hadn't planned on going to college—I was going to go in the navy 'cause that's what my dad had done, and I was going to go into electronics 'cause that's what he had done, and I was going to be a communicator 'cause that's what he had done. . . . But he [Dad's father, Jasper Garrett Sr.] said, "No, you're going to go to college. I don't know how we're going to do it—we don't have the money—but you're going to go." And I did manage to go on an Indian scholarship. They told me that I needed to study business administration 'cause at that time, that's where the scholarships were—that's how I could go to school.

But what I was really interested in was biology, so I took it and loved it! I tried to learn everything I could. And when I finally had a chance to take botany, I was in hog heaven. As a matter of fact, there are two plants in the North Carolina flora herbarium that were actually new species of plants that I identified. Usually they name the plant after the person who finds it, so I thought, *Wow! I'm going to get the plants named after me!* But actually they named them after the professor, so I learned real quick that I should've kept my mouth shut and just waited until I was a biologist or botanist so the plants could have been named after me.

So once again plants became a part of my life. Now there I was seventeen or eighteen years of age, and finally Mary came down to see me one day and said, "The medicine man wants to talk to you." And another medicine man wanted to talk to me, too; his name was William Hornbuckle. And William Hornbuckle was the one who Shirley told me would take me back into the mountains and teach me about plants. Just about everything I ever learned about plants, I learned from either Shirley or my mom or William Hornbuckle.

As an example, here I was going to school, but I was commuting and working as well. Still, every time I'd get a chance, I'd run up to see William and we would go up in the mountains. He had what he called a "sang patch," which was wild ginseng. We would walk, literally, fifteen miles back in the mountains to get to his "sang patch." And he'd say, "Nobody knows where this is—you gotta be careful 'cause there're diggers all over the place." I didn't know what a digger was until I asked Grandma. And she said, "Well, diggers are people who look for wild ginseng," 'cause they would sell it and make money off of it. I remember thinking, *Why would anybody pull up these beautiful plants just to make money?* I didn't understand that.

Anyway, we would go up the trail, and he would always take me through what he called "the wet ridges" to get up on the high side and then come down on the dry side. He would look for special plants along the way, and he'd show them to me. I didn't realize the impact of this on me until one day, when I was a junior in college, I was trying to identify all the plants that I knew. It was about sixty-five.

That may not seem like such a large number compared to the knowledge of the medicine man, who probably knew the use of and actually used some two hundred and fifty plants. But I realized that I had actually learned how to use and identify some sixty-five plants. There were some that I wouldn't necessarily use for medicine, but I did know the medicinal value of those and how to put the remedies together. You'd never pull a plant unless it was the fourth one, and you would always try to find one on the east side if there was an east side. For the north-side plants, there were certain purposes. If it was a west-side plant—in other words, one that was growing in the direction of the west—you would use it for some physical ailment. And that's the way I learned the concept of the Four Directions.

Four was a sacred number. I realized that because you'd always pick the fourth plant, always leaving three. And if there was an emergency where you really had to have a plant and there were only two there, it was OK to take the one just for that emergency purpose, as long as there was one left. If there was an emergency—say somebody was dying—and there was only one plant, you didn't take it, 'cause what was more important, the life of that person or the life of the plant? So you'd have to run around and scurry to find another patch where there would be more plants.

Now that never happened to me, but it was when I learned that, as William Hornbuckle would say, humans were the last beings to come from the spirit world, and therefore we were probably the most ignorant of all the beings. The smartest spirit beings were the plants and the animals, and there were different stages of evolution of development, which were based on spirituality. But I also learned some very natural biology lessons from William such as when he would talk about the beginning of life. He said that what existed first in the spirit world were the plants. They were to keep Mother Earth in place and make the soil fertile, so that things could grow; nothing could live until the plant spirits came first.

These were stories that taught me how important the human was on the scale of things, humans being the last to come and, certainly, the ones who had to be helped the most. This was a strong influence on me. I don't understand the attitude of some people who think that human beings are more important than animals and plants—that they can take the lives of animals or tromp all over plants and it doesn't make any difference. I remember my grandfather saying to try not to trample a plant unless you get permission to step on it, because at least that way you know you're not going to harm it and its spirit is not going to come back and harm you in any way.

A good example of that approach to life is animals being shot. Grandfather (and Uncle Ting, too) would say that when the hunters went out in the early days, when animal spirits were still closely aligned with human spirits, humans first had to get permission before they would kill them. In order to get permission, humans would have to do special ceremonies and offer tobacco to the fire, and say, "I'm going out to hunt tomorrow or this evening, and this will be a special hunting time. I'm looking for a deer, and the deer will bring meat to my family and we'll be able to use the bones for certain things." Everything was used. So the hunter would say that prayer, and then it was alright to go hunting. If the deer was killed, that was a sign that it had been OK.

But if the hunter killed the deer without giving thanks or doing the prayers, then its spirit would come and the person would end up with certain diseases. As an example, the disease inflicted by the deer spirit for violation was rheumatism. I remember seeing a man, not very old, who was all bent over, and I could tell he was hurting. I asked my uncle, "What's wrong with him?" and he said, "He's got rheumatism. He used to be a hunter, and he didn't get permission from the animals, so they gave him this disease so that for the rest of his life he'd be crippled and walking around like that."

I had no idea that I would ever be thought of as a medicine man. That was the farthest thing from my mind. But I do remember that some of the kids at school would tease me about my grandfather, who was a medicine man. My mother never called him that; she'd always say that he was just a "strong spiritual man." She'd say he went to church and was a strong spiritual man, that he knew all about hunting and animals and plants, that he was in touch with Mother Earth and knew "special things."

Some time later, I asked my grandmother about this and she said, "There was a period of time when medicine men were important people in the tribe; they were looked up to and recognized as being special, holy, and spiritual. But with the influence of the White man and modern medicine, the medicine men were looked down upon as having snake-oil cures and stuff like that."

So they lost a lot of recognition and respect among tribal members because of two influences: one was modern medicine—somebody having something this "bullet" [pill] would help or this special shot that would take the problem away. The second reason was Christianity, because, according to my grandmother, a lot of times ministers and priests would say the medicine man was doing bad things, whereas the minister or priest was doing good things—that was a strong influence. So since my grandfather was recognized in the church, it was very important for him to be recognized as a "spiritual man." But I know a lot of people would go to him for Medicine.

The next thing that happened was that I was invited to join this very special circle of people to learn the Medicine. I was the only "mixed breed"—all the rest of them were full-bloods. And I was even told one time by William Hornbuckle—he was mixed, too—that he could never be a medicine man because he was a mixed breed. He knew the herbs and he'd get them for the medicine men, and people would come to him, but he really could not call himself a medicine man because he had not gone through the orientation with one of the seven original medicine people.

I think what made my apprenticeship different is that I *did* learn under one of the last original medicine men of the tribe: Doc Amoneeta Sequoyah. I used to get teased a lot about that. People would say, "You shouldn't be spending your time with him. All he does is talk about the stuff in the past. We need to go forward and be modern."

And I didn't realize, all the years that I worked with him, even up to the time that he passed on, how important my training was with Doc Sequoyah. I went out on my own—I went into the navy during the Vietnam era. When I came out, I was going to get a job in modern industry and move out into the "real" world. But I kept being drawn back.

I just had this sense, and I had many visions come to me,

that I was to study the Medicine but that I wasn't going to be a medicine man on the reservation. I would be one who would "bridge the gap"—one to share, to help others understand and appreciate so that we could bring the integrity and reputation of Good Medicine back so that people would honor and respect and appreciate what the elders and the elder medicine people had actually brought to us. If you think about it, people survived many, many generations long before "modern medicine."

....

YOU'RE THIS AND YOU'RE THAT

As we look to the ways of the past, we begin to understand more about where we as human beings stand in relation to everything that exists around us. We begin to understand better what is in our hearts and why we are here on Mother Earth. We learn how to become the helpers that we were meant to be. The Medicine offers us, as it always has, one path among many for walking peacefully in harmony and balance upon the ground that gives us life and upon the wind that gives us breath.

So those were my influences, and if I were to choose three values that really influenced me the most from the time that I was very young until today, they would be, first of all, the sense of humility. I didn't learn that in the navy—I learned "how to play the game" in the navy. I proudly served my country, but when somebody asked if I was going to have my son go into the service so he could learn humility, I said no. I figured that you'd learn humility by being respected and showing respect for everything in life.

I never spent much time teaching you these things. What

I was supposed to do was be very subtle about that because I think I had the fear, just like I was taught, that I didn't want you to be different. I didn't want you—and Melissa [my sister]—to be chastised or criticized as being . . . different. I wanted you to be like everybody else, but I gave you very subtle influences to teach you things like humility.

And honor; that's the next value. Honoring things, honoring life, honoring animals, honoring plants—honoring everything. The third one was respect—respect for elders, respect for all things. If you put those three together, they are pretty strong values. My grandfather used to say, "If you have that, you've got it all, 'cause everything will come to you."

I think who I am is truly two people. As a matter of fact, Doc Amoneeta Sequoyah used to call me "Gagoyoti"—in other words, "two people." In Cherokee, that's a way of saying "you're this and you're that." For me, a lot of my conflicts in earlier years were because I wasn't sure who I was. Was I Indian, was I White; what was a mixture of a person; where did I belong? I knew deep down inside that I didn't belong with that class of people who felt that they were better than others. And I knew that the people I had come from, the Cherokee, were very special.

CHAPTER TWELVE

Following the Sacred Trail

In our way of life, with every decision we make, we always keep in mind the Seventh Generation of children to come. When we walk upon Mother Earth, we always plant our feet carefully, because we know that the faces of future generations are looking up at us from beneath the ground. We never forget them.

—Oren Lyons, Faithkeeper of the Onondaga Nation

I do not remember the first time I heard the saying "If you can find the end of a rainbow, you'll find a pot of gold." It sounded strange to me at the time, but it was, nonetheless, something that I tucked away somewhere in the back of my mind. After all, one never knows when one might need a pot of gold. However, as a child, it was mainly the mystery of the whole thing that struck me.

I do not remember the first time I actually saw a rainbow or where I was, but I do know that its quiet beauty struck my

169

heart with such awe that it touched something deep within me. Just seeing a rainbow catches you quite off guard and somehow just makes you stop and look . . . and wonder. I suppose it is like finding a pot of gold, although I have never had that pleasure. But I am fortunate to be able to say that I have been given many gifts during my time on Mother Earth, and seeing a rainbow has been among the more cherished of them. It is sacred.

And just as the rainbow is sacred, so is my life. Yes, my life is sacred to me. That may sound a bit arrogant at first, but only because of how it sounds rather than *what it means to me*. It is interesting when we begin to realize what we consider gifts and what we expect, what we consider privilege and what we consider obligation. For example, my mother was not obligated to give me life. And yet she did.

I remember once when I was home for my birthday, I noticed that my mother was crying to herself. When I asked her why, thinking that something had happened and maybe she needed my help, she simply responded, "I was having you right now." At first, I didn't understand. Then, I suddenly realized that she was reliving the moments leading up to my birth and that this was still such an emotionally powerful experience for her, even all these years later. She looked upon me as a gift and treated me as such. And I, in turn, have always looked upon her gift of life to me as nothing less than sacred.

I have tried to live my life with this attitude. I live my life this way because I *choose* to live my life this way. This is my Medicine, and for me it is a Good Medicine Way. It holds power for me—not the power of control, but the power of perspective. To look upon all things as sacred and purposeful is no small task for us human beings, who have been blessed with the intellectual and spiritual capacity to transcend both time and space in a single thought (sounds like Superman, right?). Yet there are times when we human beings do not choose to look beyond our noses and walk right into a tree that was standing there plain as day, for possibly hundreds of years before we arrived. "Damn trees!" we might even say.

If Uwohali, Eagle, flying high, looks no further than the end of her beak, then she misses the beauty of the great expanse that exists above, below, and all around her. The eagle who has the ability to fly but chooses not to recognize her place in relation to the Greater Circle loses that sense of place and may become lost. How might it feel to be floating high upon the wind, not knowing where we are or where we are going? Some might consider this a welcome opportunity, but for how long? When we float high upon the wind or when we walk upon the ground, can we recognize the forest for the trees? Can we even see the trees there before us, let alone the vastness of the forest of which they are a part?

Consider people's fascination with the past. What is this fascination with history, legends, stories, things from the past, and things that remind us of the past? What makes certain pictures or special gifts we received once so important to us? Are we simply burdened with too much free time, or is there a sense of connection that gives our lives meaning?

The past and things that tie us to it give us a sense of connection with those things, experiences, people that have gone before us. The Circle has no real beginning and no end; it is an extension of itself. This is powerful Medicine, and it is very sacred. In order for us to know our place in the universe, we must realize where we stand in relation to all things around us; this is the power of relation. Our connection with the past gives us a sense of continuity, a sense that we are somehow part of the Greater Circle. It gives us a sense of place and a sense of direction. Our connection with the future also gives us a sense of direction and purpose on the path that we walk.

I have long wondered what *really is* at the end of a rainbow. Quite honestly, I have never checked (I've chalked that up as one of the many pursuits for later life . . .). But I do wonder. There have been many stones on my path that I have thus far left unturned, either because I just haven't gotten around to them or maybe because those stones did not wish to be bothered in the first place (it's important to know the difference).

So every time I see a rainbow, I just stand there in awe of its beauty and immensity, and whisper a small prayer thanking the rainbow for being willing to share its beauty with me. And something about the sight of it moves me from within, as if it were touching my spirit, and a deep sense of calm comes over me. I look upon the very sight of the rainbow as a gift, just as I look upon the very sight of the eagle as a gift, and the squirrel, and the ant, and the rock, and the little dandelions, and the rain, and all living beings in the Circle of Life. I know that a rainbow is not a rainbow without all of its colors, just as the Sacred Web of Life cannot exist without every one of its strands in harmony and balance.

We usually don't look upon a rainbow and think about how much prettier the red looks than the blue or how much nicer the whole thing would be if it were curved in a different way or not curved at all. We usually either look upon the rainbow as something of great beauty in and of itself, or we may just ignore it almost altogether. The point is, when we look upon something as a gift, we tend to accept it as it is, to appreciate it as it is, and it just makes us feel good. There is a sense of connection. It touches something within us and somehow grants us sacred moments of harmony.

· ·

OWNING THE SKY

Being thankful is an important part of the Medicine. In the traditional Cherokee Way, when children argued over an object, it was taken away from them and they were then encouraged to lie down on Mother Earth and look up at the sky. While observing the sky, the children were reminded that focusing attention on an object and on wanting to possess that object removed them from the harmony and balance of the Greater Circle. Then the children were asked to focus their attention on Father Sky. "Look at the sky. . . . Can you see the clouds?" the children might be asked. "Watch the way they move and change before your eyes. Can you see pictures in the clouds? Can you see the spirit people there?"

The focus of the children's attention with possessing something was replaced with the openness of the sky and the movement of all our relations in Galun'lati, or the Above World, such as the clouds, the wind, the birds. "Should we seek to own the sky?" it might have been asked. A renewed sense of relation and clarity was sought for the children as they were asked to open their minds and hearts to the movement and language of the cloud people, who speak in shapes and pictures.

The children might then have been asked to help out with a particular task as a way of replacing "wanting" thoughts with "giving" thoughts. This was only one of many ways in which to encourage openness, creativity, and humility in the presence of all Creation. This was a very important experience for helping young people (and some adults) to understand the power of relation and the sense of humility required to live in harmony and balance with all living beings in the Circle. True wisdom comes to us when we let go of the attachments that bind us and draw upon the sacred Medicine of all our relations. This, too, is Good Medicine.

THE SACRED ART OF GIVEAWAY

As North Americans, we like to remind ourselves to be thankful for what we *receive*, and we try to remind our children to be that way as well. We associate such special times of the year as Thanksgiving with being thankful for what we have received during the year and during our lives (I had a friend who jokingly called it "Thanks-taking"). Yet, in the Cherokee Way, it is also very important to be thankful for what we have to *give*. Think about all the things you have to give or do give maybe every day or at certain special times.

As mentioned in chapter 5, in the Native tradition of the "Giveaway," something is willingly given up or distributed to others as a way of celebrating and maintaining the harmony and balance of the Circle. It is a way of reaffirming one's connection with the natural flow of the Greater Circle of Life through an expression of wisdom, kindness, and humility—and without the expectation of receiving something in return other than the honor of being able to "gift" someone.

Giveaway is based in the idea that what we consider to be possessions are indeed never truly "owned" by anyone and must eventually pass to another or be returned to Mother Earth; in a sense, we are only caretakers. Giveaway also emphasizes a sense of appreciation and humility, and the importance of reciprocity through receiving and giving in turn. In the traditional way, it is believed that every person and every thing has at least one special gift to offer the rest of Creation. This is not something that makes us better than anyone or anything else, but something we have to give that makes us *a part of* everyone and everything else around us by honoring the relationship.

EXERCISE: Giveaway

Think of someone who is very special to you. It may be a family member, a friend, even an acquaintance. Now think of one of the most valued possessions that you have, one that you feel would be greatly appreciated by that person for whatever reason. How about just giving it away to that person? This is Giveaway.

However, Giveaway doesn't necessarily mean the giving of material possessions. It might be the giving of kind words or a comforting touch, or somehow helping someone or something when they need it most. It is the giving of our time, our energy, our Medicine, our prayers, our love. Even our smile is sacred and should be shared whenever possible. To stir the spirit of joy in others is also powerful Medicine. Even if we have nothing else to give, we always have a smile. And that is worth more than all the riches in the world.

The real meaning of Giveaway reflects kindness and respect for all our brothers and sisters. It leads us to a path of Good Medicine and brings, in return, a gift of feelings that are often difficult to describe. It is not the worth of the gift itself, but the worth of the *gift of sharing* that is planted as a seed in the heart of another, as we continue to honor the Circle of Life.

....

HONORING THE CIRCLE

When one is receiving, it is only natural to continue the Circle by giving in turn. Think of someone who has helped you out in some way even though they didn't have to, especially someone who has helped you when you really needed it. Where would you be right now if that person hadn't helped you? Opening up to all our relations and the energy of the Circle means being able to share as well as receive and to do so in creative and meaningful ways. That is the way of the Circle.

And it is important to give to those who appreciate what you offer and let go of those who do not. There is no purpose in holding on to people whose lessons may lie in a different direction. When and if they are ready to walk the path of harmony and balance, they will return. Otherwise, it is our respectful obligation to let them go in their own way. We cannot choose for someone else, and they do not have the right to harm our spirit. Gather everything in the palms of your hands. Look at what is worth keeping and blow the rest away with a breath of kindness.

We all have choice. However, in the traditional way, one never takes without giving something in turn. This is a way of the Circle known as "balancing things," and this is Osda Nuwati, or Good Medicine. If we go out into our natural surroundings to take a particular plant, for instance, there are certain ways of going about this so as not to disturb the harmony and balance, as my father recounted in chapter 11. As we walk, we respectfully inform Nature of our intentions, and when we have found what it is that we need, we make an offering of some sort, maybe a little tobacco or whatever is appropriate. We tell the little plants why it is that we need their help, and we ask their permission for their willingness to come with us. We do not take the first one, or the second, or even the third one, but only the fourth one out of respect for the plants. As always, we say a little prayer of thanks to the plants and to the Creator, taking only what we need. As we go, we offer *our* help in whatever way we can; maybe there is some trash that could be picked up, so the little plants won't be crowded out of their homes. There is always something that we can do to be of service to our relatives in nature.

This idea of balancing things serves a very special purpose in the Circle of Life. It is as a river of kindness that flows through the Circle with much energy. In our lives, we must not be so concerned with what we're trying to accomplish that we forget our true purpose of being helpers, or caretakers. If we view ourselves as helpers first and foremost, we are taking our place in the Sacred Circle and we are living in a Good Medicine Way, no matter who we are or where we come from. Here's a good rule of thumb: For every person who helps you, it is your willing obligation to help seven others in turn. And they too, must help seven others, and so on and so forth. In this way, the Circle of Life turns with the spirit of generosity and kindness. That is the way of the Circle, and it is Good Medicine for all living beings.

···

AND THE CIRCLE TURNS

We are connected with all things, and we need only discover this truth to discover the power and beauty of relation that flows through the Circle. In the Cherokee Way, we call upon all our relations for strength, guidance, wisdom, and protection. We call upon our relations for comfort and for sharing. There is harmony and balance in the energy of our connections.

All things are alive and have spirit. All things have a purpose in this world, and all things are deserving of the respect and kindness we would give to any brother or sister. It is up to us to really listen and to "feel" the connection that we have with all our relations, including the plants and the trees, or "tree people;" the animals as our four-legged brothers and sisters; the birds, or "winged ones;" the fish, the little insects, and all the rocks and minerals, or "rock people;" the ground upon which we walk, or "Mother Earth;" the winds, or "Four Powers;" the rain and the "cloud people;" "Father Sky," "Grandfather Sun" and "Grandmother Moon," and "The Red Thunder Beings." We are members of this sacred family, and we, too, have an honored place in the Circle.

We give thanks to the Great One, to each of the Four Directions, to Father Sky, to Mother Earth, and to all our relations for all the gifts that we receive. All of these things have life of their own, and all of these things are sacred. Each one has a special reason for existing and a sacred purpose to fulfill in the greater scheme of things. Each one has a lesson to offer us if we just take the time to watch and listen, and to feel the spirit of our brothers and sisters. Each one represents a single strand in the Web of Life or a single color in a rainbow of many, many colors. All of these things are to be respected as a special part of the Greater Circle of Life. And it is the "relation" of each part to the others that creates a special flow in the energy called "life," through harmony and balance. Therefore, we look to each of the Four Directions and give thanks.

In the direction of the East, Grandfather Sun rises each day, once again bathing us in his warmth and light. As the night sky fades into the west and Sun renews his path along the skyvault, we are again reminded of the Circle, ongoing, everlasting. Young flowers bend themselves toward the brightness and open their petals to receive Sun's life energy. The little plants embrace the sunlight as they welcome the new day. In the traditional way, we also greet Grandfather Sun every morning, giving thanks. Every day, we acknowledge his warmth and light as everything on Mother Earth grows strong and flourishes in his beauty. Grandfather Sun is sacred and so, too, is his child, the Sacred Fire.

Every day, we can acknowledge the beauty in every living thing by taking the time to notice it. The same is true of our relations with other people. We should acknowledge the warmth and light in everyone. We can acknowledge the Sacred Fire in every living thing. We all share much in common no matter who we are or where we come from. We are all part of the same family.

In the direction of the South, we give thanks for the natural beauty of the plants, the trees, all the greenery that gives us food to eat, shelter to protect us, tools for our survival. Mother Earth has been around since the beginning of time. She has undergone many changes, and she has endured with great splendor and mystery. We, human beings, have been around for a long time, too. And we have survived only because of the attention that Mother Earth devotes to us, her children, providing us with all the things that we need to live and grow.

We, too, must give our attention to Mother Earth as she requires nurturing and care. It is important for us to find time every once in awhile to just go out and spend some time with Mother Earth, even if only for fifteen minutes or so. It is important for us to thank our Mother for the gift of life and appreciate all of her beauty. As always, it is good for us to give thanks for the gifts we receive and to give something in return, no matter how great or small.

In the direction of the West, we are reminded of the sound of raindrops falling on leaves—raindrops falling to the ground, gently, steadily. We can hear the soothing sound of the rain in our minds; we can feel the cleansing in our hearts. We are reminded of the still surface and wondrous beauty of ponds and lakes. We can, at once, see our reflections in the surface and the depths of what lies beneath. We are reminded of the sound of a mountain river rushing over heavy rocks and the feel of a soft mist on our faces from the river's steady motion. We can hear the river singing its ancient song.

The sacred element of Water is purifying and healing in its gentleness and its infinite strength. Water quenches our thirst. It cleanses our body, mind, and spirit of toxins, and it gives of itself in all ways so that we may live. When we once grew inside our mothers, we were surrounded by the comfort of Water. The spirit of Water is that of purity, and it reminds us of the importance of appreciating and embracing the natural flow. It reminds us that we, too, are liquid beings (our bodies are some 80 percent water) who must flow in order to be in our best Medicine. Water is one of the most powerful elements because of its ability to absorb such enormous amounts of energy. We also have the ability to embrace the energy of all things and to value the energy that makes every living thing unique and strong in its own way.

In the direction of the North, we listen to the quiet of Wind carrying our thoughts forth. When we are born, Wind gives us our first breath. From that time on, Wind is always with us as we inhale and exhale, inhale and exhale. We are, during our time on Mother Earth, forever receiving and giving back. So, too, Wind enters our bodies, our minds, and our spirits, bringing solitude and strength, and then leaves us, taking uncertainty and fear with it, transforming this disharmony into gentle energy.

Right now, inhale deeply as you count to four, then slowly exhale, counting backward from seven. Do this four times, and give thanks each time. The spirit of Wind is that of calm and quiet—wisdom. Wind is most generous in its movements; it breathes life upon all things and carries away destructive energies, replacing them with a sense of stillness. Just as Wind breathes life into us, we have the ability to breath life into those around us by allowing our gentleness and kindness to show through and embrace our relations.

With each of the directions, we are reminded of our interrelationship with all things. We must acknowledge and encourage our interdependence with all our relations for the Circle of Life to continue in harmony and balance. We have the opportunity to give thanks for all the gifts that we receive in the way that we live and the way of life that we choose. Like all living beings, we have a sacred place in the Circle, and we always have something to give. It is up to us to discover what that is. It is up to us to know our Medicine and to use it for the benefit of the Circle and all our relations.

....

THE NATURE OF THE JOURNEY

Earlier, I spoke of the Medicine that rainbows hold for me; I spoke of the rainbow as a part of the journey. We can speak of the rainbow as a refraction of light and color, or we can speak of the rainbow as spirit energy. In the same way, we can speak of our own minds as the sky, our own thoughts as spirit energy refracted at will to reflect the beauty and color of our hearts, the power of relation that flows through our veins, and the vision that keeps us oriented along the journey. We can speak of the light as the energy that we all share in common with all our relations: life!

And now I ask, what if I did finally go looking for the end of a rainbow as I mentioned that I still intend to do, and what if I were lucky enough to find it? What if, when I finally found the end of the rainbow, there was no pot of gold waiting there for me? Would I say, "Damn rainbows!" and kick the rainbow because I didn't get what I expected? Would I just give up? Would rainbows be any less beautiful to me? Would I go looking for another rainbow to follow? Would I simply look elsewhere (perhaps at the end of a tornado) for my pot of gold? What would I do? I suppose it all depends upon what I am really looking for and why, as well as how I go about it.

Now, think about yourself. What are you really looking for? Where is your sense of place? What is it that moves you? What are the things you cherish? What are the gifts that you have received, and what are the gifts that you have to give? Where is your love? Where does your vision lead you? What will it take for you to follow your vision?

The journey is not "somewhere over there" or "some other time." It is with us right here and right now. It is a part of us in everything that we do and everything that we are. What we perceive as our "pot of gold" may in fact be something very different when and if we find the end of the rainbow. What if the rainbow has no end? What if it is a circle that wraps itself gently around Earth in a continuous cycle of energy?

As we walk, all of our ancestors walk with us. As we dance, all of our ancestors dance the Sacred Dance. Each step that we place is an important one. All of our relatives are walking with us, speaking through us like the many colors of the rainbow. Listen, and you will hear their steps, their voices, their colors. Listen, and you will hear your spirit calling upon all our relations, and you will feel their energy. Our spirit is an extension of them and they are an extension of us. Our spirit connects us with the memories of all that has gone before us, all that is, and all that will be. Our spirit connects us with all of our relations in the Circle of Life. Listen, and you will hear Water speaking, Wind dancing, Sun smiling, the heartbeat of Mother Earth pulsing beneath our feet.

Every footstep is the journey. Every sight, every sound, every touch and taste and smell with which we are blessed is the journey. All of the colors before us are the journey, and *we* are the journey. May we always keep our feet on Mother Earth, our eyes and minds above the treetops, our spirit with the Greater Universal Spirit. And may we always walk the path of Good Medicine in harmony and balance, with a sense of humility, kindness, wonder, and respect for all living things as we follow the sacred trail of those who have come before us and those yet to come.

CHAPTER THIRTEEN

Touch the Earth, Taste the Wind

The center of the universe is everywhere.
—BLACK ELK, OGLALA LAKOTA MEDICINE MAN

ach of us is searching for something that we know as "home," something that we *feel* is home. Some of us are closer to it than others. Home is something that we know when we are there and long for when we are away from there. Home is not necessarily a particular physical place. It is a place of connection in the heart that is full of belonging. Home is with certain objects or things; it is with certain places and certain people. Home is with certain memories that will never be lost to us, even as we cross over breathlessly into the world beyond.

Home is something that changes as we change. It is a feeling. It is a place where we are at peace with things, where we are safe and open to whatever needs to happen. Some of us fight going home because we are not ready. Some of us stumble across home without meaning to. Some of us look for home in one place only to find that home was somewhere completely different, and we learn. Home is a feeling of warmth. It is a moment of truth that transcends all time.

And so, as we live our lives, we learn about home and we learn about ourselves. Home is a story . . . the story of our life. Home is a way. Home is a medicine song carried forth into the depths of the silence of the night, beneath the tender glow of Moon, and further beyond into the rising orangey glow of her lover, Sun, as they come together in harmony and balance.

Home is all that which feels familiar and comfortable, and inspires us to always and forever be more than we are. Home makes our spirit glow and flow. Home makes our spirit shimmer like a rainbow that hangs in the sky, offering itself there in slow motion for all to enjoy, at least for those who will take the time to notice . . .

Home is the silent dream of a child, wishing, hoping, creating . . . unlimited by the fears and emptiness of those who turn away from the pulsing heartbeat, Nuwati, and the infinite beauty of our Great Creation. Home is the first smile of an infant cradled lovingly in its parents' arms. Home is the touch and reassuring smile of one who is always there at the right time, no matter what. No matter what. Home is the ground upon which we walk, which has always been there for us and always offers herself to us tenderly; the land and the people are one. The spirit never dies.

The Medicine Way is the way of life. It is the way of humility, of giving, of loving, and of thankfulness. As you walk your journey, do not forget to touch Elohino, Mother Earth. As you walk, let your footsteps fall lightly upon the ground. Come down upon your knees, press your hands gently upon her body, and feel her heart beating against your palms. Do not forget what she feels like, what she looks like, what she smells like, what she sounds like. Listen closely to her humming an ancient song that needs no words—softly, quietly. She will never ask you to come to her because that is not her way. She asks for nothing and offers everything.

And she is always glad to see you when you come to her, and sometimes she cries tears of joy to see her little baby once again, no matter what. No matter what. And her tears flow freely, cleansing all that is. Let her tears flow against your skin, cool and sure. Do not forget what she feels like. She is your mother.

And whether you have found home or whether you are looking for home, it is good to be thankful. What is it that has power for you? What is it that holds beauty for you? What is it that gives you peace? What is it that carries a sense of joy for you? The Sacred Fire glows eternally in our hearts. And for this, we have much to be thankful.

I carry with me a little Cherokee prayer that my father taught me when I was young; I carry it in my spirit. I don't even know when I learned it or how I came to know it, yet it is always with me and will never leave me because it is in my spirit. I speak it silently when I am giving thanks for food or for time with friends and family, to be blessed with the sight and experience of another day; when I feel home and when I am far from home; when I touch Mother Earth; and when I walk upon the wind—and, always, I taste the wind slowly, surely, evenly.

These are my words of life. These are my words of truth. I speak the words, and this is my breath of life, being taken in and offered forth. All things are connected. I offer the gift of a little sacred tobacco as I speak the words and give thanks that the four winds will carry my thoughts and my prayers where they need to go. Let the fire be lighted.

Ogedoda	O Great One
Galun'lati	who dwells in the Sky World
Ogadosgi	illuminating all that is,
Osda Nuwati	giving Good Medicine of life
Elohino	and the Great Creation, our Mother Earth,
Yolda	knowing that all things are as they should be,
Hoyona	we give thanks for the beauty of all things, O Great One,
Wah doh	we give thanks.

Bibliography

Bradley, R.K. *Weavers of Tales: A Collection of Cherokee Legends.* Cherokee, NC: Betty Dupree, 1967.

Brendtro, L.K., M. Brokenleg, and S. Van Bockern. *Reclaiming Youth at Risk: Our Hope for the Future.* Bloomington, IN: National Education Service, 1990.

Chief Seattle. *How Can One Sell the Air?: A Manifesto for the Earth.* Summertown, TN: Book Publishing Company, 1988.

Commoner, B. *The Closing Circle.* New York: Bantam, 1971.

Craven, M. *I Heard the Owl Call My Name.* New York: Laurel, 1973.

Deloria Jr., V. *God is Red: A Native View of Religion.* Golden, CO: Fulcrum, 1994.

Earth Works Group. *50 Simple Things You Can Do to Save the Earth.* Berkeley, CA: Earthworks, 1989.

Garrett, J.T. "Where the Medicine Wheel Meets Medical Science." *Profiles in Wisdom: Native Elders Speak About the Earth*, edited by S. McFadden. Santa Fe, NM: Bear & Company, 1991.

Garrett, J.T. and M.T. Garrett. *Medicine of the Cherokee: The Way of Right Relationship.* Santa Fe, NM: Bear & Company, 1996.

Garrett, M.T. and J.E. Myers. "The Rule of Opposites: A Paradigm for Counseling Native Americans." *Journal of Multicultural Counseling and Development* 24 (1996): 89-104.

Goldberg, B. *Past Lives, Future Lives.* New York: Ballantine, 1997.

Hifler, J.S. *A Cherokee Feast of Days: Daily Meditations.* Tulsa, OK: Council Oak, 1992.

Jones, A. "From Fragmentation to Wholeness: A Green Approach to Science and Society." Part 1. *The Ecologist* 17, no. 6 (1987): 236-240.

———. "From Fragmentation to Wholeness: A Green Approach to Science and Society." Part 2. *The Ecologist* 18, no. 1 (1988): 30-34.

Lake, (Robert) Medicine Grizzlybear. *Native Healer: Initiation into an Ancient Art.* Wheaton, IL: Quest, 1991.

Locust, C. "Wounding the Spirit: Discrimination and Traditional American Indian Belief Systems." *Harvard Educational Review* 58 , no. 3 (1988): 315-330.

McFadden, S., ed. *The Little Book of Native American Wisdom*. Rockport, MA: Element, 1994.

——. *Profiles in Wisdom: Native Elders Speak about the Earth*. Santa Fe, NM: Bear & Co., 1991

Neihardt, J.G. *Black Elk Speaks: Being the Life Story of a Holy Man of the Oglala Sioux*. New York: Pocket, 1959.

Oswalt, W.H. *This Land Was Theirs: A Study of North American Indians*. 4th ed. Mountain View, CA: Mayfield, 1988.

Reed, M. *Seven Clans of the Cherokee Society*. Cherokee, NC: Cherokee Publications, 1993.

Sun Bear, C. Mulligan, P. Nufer, and Wabun. *Walk in Balance: The Path to Healthy, Happy, Harmonious Living*. New York: Simon & Schuster, 1989.

Wilson Schaef, A. *Native Wisdom for White Minds*. New York: Ballantine, 1995.

Ywahoo, D. *Voices of Our Ancestors: Cherokee Teachings from the Wisdom Fire*. Boston: Shambhala, 1987.

About the Author

Michael Tlanusta Garrett, Eastern Band of Cherokee, is an assistant professor of counselor education at the University of North Carolina at Charlotte. He holds a Ph.D. in counselor education and an M.Ed. in counseling and development from the University of North Carolina at Greensboro. Author/coauthor of numerous articles and book chapters, he has co-written with his father, J.T. Garrett, *Medicine of the Cherokee: The Way of Right Relationship*, also published by Bear & Company (1996).

Michael's experience with Native people, both professionally and personally, lends a unique perspective and expertise with Native American issues and concerns. Michael has worked with children and adolescents in the schools, with Native American and other minority students in higher education, as an individual and group therapist in a community agency setting, and as a project director in an urban Indian center serving the local Indian community. During the past several years, he has taught courses at the university level and given numerous presentations, workshops, and seminars on topics including wellness, cultural values and beliefs, spirituality, relationships, group techniques, counseling children, conflict resolution, date rape / sexual violence, and play therapy.

Michael grew up on the Cherokee Indian Reservation in the mountains of western North Carolina.

BOOKS OF RELATED INTEREST

MEDICINE OF THE CHEROKEE
The Way of Right Relationship
by J. T. Garrett and Michael Garrett

THE CHEROKEE FULL CIRCLE
A Practical Guide to Sacred Ceremonies and Traditions
by J. T. Garrett, Ed.D., and Michael Tlanusta Garrett, Ph.D.

THE CHEROKEE HERBAL
Native Plant Medicine from the Four Directions
by J. T. Garrett

MEDITATIONS WITH THE CHEROKEE
Prayers, Songs, and Stories of Healing and Harmony
by J. T. Garrett

THE CHEROKEE SACRED CALENDAR
A Handbook of the Ancient Native American Tradition
by Raven Hail

LEGENDS AND PROPHECIES OF THE QUERO APACHE
Tales for Healing and Renewal
by Maria Yracébûrû

MEDITATIONS WITH THE NAVAJO
Prayers, Songs, and Stories of Healing and Harmony
by Gerald Hausman

MEDITATIONS WITH THE HOPI
by Robert Boissiere

THE MAN WHO KNEW THE MEDICINE
The Teachings of Bill Eagle Feather
by Henry Niese

GIFT OF POWER
The Life and Teachings of a Lakota Medicine Man
by Archie Fire Lame Deer and Richard Erdoes

CRYING FOR A DREAM
The World through Native American Eyes
by Richard Erdoes

THE LAKOTA SWEAT LODGE CARDS
Spiritual Teachings of the Sioux
by Chief Archie Fire Lame Deer and Helene Sarkis

SUN DANCING
A Spiritual Journey on the Red Road
by Michael Hull

MEDITATIONS WITH THE LAKOTA
Prayers, Songs, and Stories of Healing and Harmony
New Edition of Meditations with Native Americans
by Paul Steinmetz

TWO RAVENS
The Life and Teachings of a Spiritual Warrior
by Louis Two Ravens Irwin and Robert Liebert

CALL OF THE GREAT SPIRIT
The Shamanic Life and Teachings of Medicine Grizzly Bear
by Bobby Lake-Thom

Inner Traditions • Bear & Company
P.O. Box 388
Rochester, VT 05767
1-800-246-8648
www.InnerTraditions.com

Or contact your local bookseller